WHAT EVER

WHAT EVERY
SMALL GROUP
LEADER
SHOULD KNOW

Larry Kreider

Regal

From Gospel Light
Ventura, California, U.S.A.

Published by Regal
From Gospel Light
Ventura, California, U.S.A.
www.regalbooks.com
Printed in the U.S.A.

Note: Some of the names in this book have been changed
to honor those whose stories are being told, while other stories
are a composite of real-life stories.

Library of Congress Cataloging-in-Publication Data
Kreider, Larry.
What every small-group leader should know / Larry Kreider.
p. cm.
ISBN 978-0-8307-5327-7 (trade paper)
1. Church group work. 2. Small groups—Religious aspects—Christianity.
I. Title.
BV652.2.K74 2010
253'.7—dc22
2010013051

Rights for publishing this book outside the U.S.A. or in non-English
languages are administered by Gospel Light Worldwide, an international
not-for-profit ministry. For additional information, please visit
www.glww.org, email info@glww.org, or write to Gospel Light Worldwide,
1957 Eastman Avenue, Ventura, CA 93003, U.S.A.

To order copies of this book and other Regal products in bulk quantities,
please contact us at 1-800-446-7735.

*This book is dedicated to the thousands
of ordinary believers in Christ who are on an
extraordinary mission as they obey the call to
serve others through small-group ministry.*

CONTENTS

ACKNOWLEDGMENTS

A special thanks to Karen Ruiz, my editor and writing assistant, who helped gather and organize the material for this book from what we have learned and experienced during four decades of small-group ministry. Thanks also to Peter Bunton, Joe Nolt, Steve Prokopchak, Brian Sauder and Ron Myer, who read through the manuscript and offered significant feedback. Thanks to Kim Bangs, Gary Greig, Deena Davis and Mark Weising from Regal Books for their valuable insights, editing and encouragement. And thanks to all the small-group leaders and ministry colleagues whose valuable input over the years has contributed to doing what Jesus told us to do—make disciples from house to house as every believer helps others grow spiritually.

INTRODUCTION

Leading a small group gives you the opportunity to invest in someone else's life! You don't have to be a great leader or a dynamic teacher to lead a small group; God is more interested in your availability. To borrow the famous first line from Rick Warren's book *The Purpose Driven Life*, "It's not about you!" It's about what God can do through you as you minimize yourself and magnify God.

Whether you currently lead a small group that is a ministry of your congregation, or you want to start a small group and need a field-tested tool to assist you on your journey, this book will help you along the way.

I wish I'd had this book 40 years ago when I first began to lead small groups. I would have saved myself much grief. But I am happy to share with you what I have learned about small-group leadership and small-group dynamics, including the mistakes I have made (so you don't have to make the same mistakes). I am convinced that healthy small groups are God's strategy for us to experience true community while practically helping others and learning to be true disciples of Jesus Christ.

The first small group I led was at a youth group retreat in northern Pennsylvania. Although I was a fairly new believer in Christ, the youth leaders had enough confidence in me to trust me to lead my first small group. Looking back now, it has been an amazing privilege to lead more small groups than I can count, and help start many churches and ministries worldwide. Moreover, it has been a great honor to be asked to train Christian leaders throughout the nations, from dozens of denominations, and many churches and ministries, in healthy small-group ministry. I am so glad I took that first step of faith 40 years ago. It prepared me for my journey in learning to lead small groups.

If you are leading a Bible study, a home group, a small group, a Sunday School class at your church, a discipleship group with a college campus ministry or a new house church in your community, this book is for you. It is filled with practical, biblical and field-tested insights on small-group ministry that will assist you in the days ahead. You will understand as you read through the following pages that small-group ministry is much more than having good meetings. The focus must be on helping every person in the small group become conformed to the image of Christ. May God bless you as you read and as you embark on this journey of leading healthy small groups for the glory of God.

CHAPTER 1

MY STORY: LEARNING TO LEAD A SMALL GROUP THE HARD WAY

God Calls Ordinary People to Lead Small Groups

My history with small groups spans more than four decades. After initially leading a few small groups in our church youth group in Pennsylvania, and then as a 21-year-old newlywed, serving as a missionary for one year with my wife, LaVerne, I was ready for the next step in my journey with God. I returned to Pennsylvania to work on my father's farm and serve as a volunteer in our local Mennonite church. During the summer of 1971, I served along with LaVerne and a team of young leaders, and launched a ministry from our church to reach the unchurched youth in our south-central Pennsylvania community. I was a chicken farmer at the time, with a calling to reach my world for Christ. We played sports and conducted assorted clubs throughout the week for spiritually needy youngsters and teenagers. This kind of friendship evangelism produced results, and during the next few years, dozens of young people came to faith in Christ.

We transported the kids who we were mentoring to many of the churches in our community, because we wanted to help them find a church. But they just didn't seem to fit in. These youth actually preferred the non-churchy, spontaneous atmosphere they experienced in our home where we often met in small groups for times of prayer, praise and informal Bible studies and outreach.

We found that new Christians need a new structure (or new wineskin[1]) that is flexible and pliable. They will thrive when placed in a small group that encourages their spiritual growth.

The Underground Church

One day in 1978, while praying, I was startled when I heard the Lord speak to me through His still, small voice. He said, "Are you willing to be involved in the underground church?" The words were clear, and even though I didn't quite understand what God was trying to tell me, I told Him that I was willing.

In a short span of time, I began to understand what the Lord was requiring of me. He helped me realize there was a need in the church for small groups that would be flexible enough to relate to believers from all backgrounds and assist them in their spiritual growth. These small groups were to be the "underground" part of the church. God was calling me, along with a team of others, to start a new church based on small groups—an underground church, if you will. It would be like a tree that shows its trunk, branches and leaves. But that is only half of the picture. The unnoticed half, the underground root system, nourishes the whole tree and keeps it healthy. When the part of the church that is underground is strong, then the whole church would be strong and continue to grow.

Just as water and nutrients feed a tree through its root system, so too the church is nourished and strengthened by what happens in the underground, or the unseen realm of church life—believers involved in small groups. This new wineskin, or model of church structure, could be tailor-made to serve the new believers in Jesus Christ.

After months of concentrated prayer and receiving counsel from various church leaders, we were released, with blessing, from our local church so that we could start this new church built on small groups. Our leaders prayed publicly for God's blessing to be upon us as we took this step of faith. We called the new church DOVE Christian Fellowship. Initially, we met in three small groups during the week and held a larger gathering on Sunday mornings.

There was a sense of excitement among us as we met in three separate home groups during the week, pursuing the vision the Lord had given us. But there were also times of pain. Within the first year, the three original small groups became two. Instead of the groups growing and multiplying, it seemed like we were going backward. We soon realized that we had a lack of clear leadership for the groups, which caused confusion. We found ourselves in the "School of the Holy Spirit," often learning the hard way. We were learning basic principles and insights for leading healthy small groups, which I will share with you throughout this book.

Servant Leadership

We had encouraged the believers in the first small groups not to designate any one person as a leader, but instead to choose a team that would provide coequal leadership. This partly stemmed from the uncertainty of many of our young group even to think that they might possess a gift of leadership. Many had never been in leadership roles and hesitated to see themselves as an actual leader.

We soon realized that the growth of the groups and the individuals within the groups would be stunted unless there was clear, God-appointed leadership. The leaders needed to be loving servant-leaders who desired to build a leadership team and, above all, they needed to be leaders called by God. True spiritual fathers and mothers are needed who really care about the people in the group. People will give themselves to a task when they know there is clear, God-given, loving leadership.

At the time, however, we were ignorant of these dynamics, so we appointed each small group with coequal leaders (the church at large was led by six coequal leaders). Within the first year, this "leaderless group" came to the difficult realization that there was a desperate need for clear leadership among us. Although we continued to believe that team leadership was important, we recognized the need for "headship" within each leadership team.

In light of this important discovery, we appointed, and our denomination ordained, two leaders from the original group of six co-leaders. I was acknowledged as the primary leader of the church leadership team. Additionally, each small group was encouraged to find a leader who would actively cooperate with the Holy Spirit to become a fellow worker with God (see 1 Cor. 3:9). They were encouraged to develop a team of leaders to serve with them in each small group. As novice leaders, we were stretched in our abilities and made lots of mistakes, but God was faithful.

During the 10 years following our church's bumpy start, it grew to well over 2,000 believers scattered throughout communities in a seven-county area of southeastern Pennsylvania. These believers met in more than 100 small groups during the week and on Sunday mornings in five different congregations. The whole church came together in a large gymnasium or a local park amphitheater five or six times each year, for a combined corporate celebration.

Whenever clusters of small groups (congregations) that were renting facilities for Sunday morning "celebrations" outgrew a building, we either moved to a larger building or started two or three celebration meetings in the same building on a Sunday. But the focus was not on the Sunday morning meetings. The focus was on the church meeting from house to house in small groups each week throughout our communities.

Our goal was to continue to lead people to Christ, multiply the small groups and celebrations and begin new Sunday morning celebrations and new small groups in other areas as we increased in numbers. We also found that by renting buildings at an economical price, we had more money available to use for world missions. During these years, churches were planted in Scotland, Brazil and Kenya. These overseas churches were built on Jesus Christ and on these same underground house-to-house principles.

Learning the Hard Way

Unfortunately, the storms began to mount. There seemed to be a constant undercurrent that sapped me, and the others in leadership, of strength and vision. It was subtle—happening without us even realizing what was taking place—and it was hard to put our finger on it. I found myself increasingly making decisions that were based more on the desires of others than on what I really believed was the Lord's direction for us as a church. Small-group leaders were feeling the same thing. We found ourselves becoming more and more distracted by the many voices around us.

We even fell into a trap of adopting methods we had seen work in other churches, even though the Lord had not called us to those methods. We learned the hard way that it is of utmost importance to adopt Christ's value system and hear from Him and Him alone for the direction to take as a church. We were continuing to learn lifelong principles that applied to small-group ministry.

During the spring of 1991, we took time to pray and reevaluate. As we continued to seek God's face, we started to understand what the Lord was trying to tell us.

Change Is Inevitable in Small Groups

A basic aspect of small groups is that change is inevitable, even desirable! The good thing about change is that it often provides an opportunity to learn to trust the sovereignty of God more fully.

As we continued to pursue the vision and call God had given us—to build the underground church (small groups) around the world—it became clearer that in order for us to accomplish that vision, we needed to be willing to "give the church away."

How do you give a church away? When our oldest daughter, Katrina, was married, we realized we had spent

21 years giving her our time, resources, love, encouragement and finances. Then, we became aware that we had made this investment in her to give her away to a young man who would be her husband. We had trained her to give her away.

The Lord is calling us to train and invest in His people to give them away! That's another important concept to understand in healthy small-group ministry. We cannot control and hold on to those in our group; we must train them and release them to fulfill God's purposes. We need to live with the expectation that many of the believers in our small groups and churches will eventually have their own families (new small groups and possibly plant new churches). It's in our best interest to train people so that we can give them away. The same concept that applies to natural families applies to spiritual families. We train our children to one day become healthy adults who support their own vision and family. As parents, we must be willing to give them away and not hold on to them.

We recognized that the Lord had called us to be an international family of churches and ministries, and we began to take steps to make the transition. Our new family of churches and ministries would have a common focus: a mandate from God to plant and establish small groups and church-planting movements throughout the world.

Our Transition to a New Model

As a small-group-based church-planting movement, we were intent on training a new generation of small-group leaders, church planters and other Christian leaders. So, a family of self-governing churches better suited our goal of mobilizing and empowering God's people. In this way, everyone—individuals, families, small groups and congregations—could fulfill His purposes at the grassroots level.

We believe small groups should have a God-given vision to plant new small groups. We also believe that every congregation should have a God-given vision to plant new churches. This gives all of us a chance to spread our wings and fly!

On January 1, 1996, after more than two years of preparing for transition, our small-group-based church in Pennsylvania became eight self-governed churches, each with its own eldership team. Our overseas churches followed suit. We formed a leadership council to give spiritual oversight to DOVE Christian Fellowship International (DCFI), and I was asked to serve as its international director.

Small groups provide our basic structure as we seek to reach out beyond ourselves to make disciples for Jesus Christ. Intercession is a priority as we realize that the struggles God's people face are not with flesh and blood, but with principalities and powers in heavenly places (see Eph. 6:12). As small groups are constantly growing and multiplying, leadership training is a very important part of our mission.

Experience Community

When people experience a loving community in a small group, they find the group to be a nurturing place, a place of support. The small group provides a safe place to deal with pain and grow spiritually. Building relationships within small groups moves beyond superficial social contacts to serving each other out of reverence for Christ. In small groups we learn to truly love one another, forgive one another, bear each other's burdens and be generous in hospitality.

Kelly, who was divorced and the mother of two children, experienced the love and care of her small group during a difficult time in her life. She had let the insurance lapse on her car, and because of an earlier accident, she was notified that her license, tags and registration were being suspended for three months. Her job as a school bus driver was in jeopardy. How would she provide for her daughters? She asked her small group to pray. With that, she sensed that God had something really big planned for her during her three months out of a job.

On her last day of work, she came home to three very large and full bags of groceries. The next three months were more of the same. People in her small group offered to help. She had rides everywhere! A frozen turkey with all the trimmings showed up at her doorstep for Thanksgiving dinner. Her fuel and doctor bills were paid, and Christmas was taken care of, with food and gifts for the children. Kelly learned that God provides, and He provided often through His people in her small group, who had become her friends. A very important part of small groups involves caring for those in the group.

Despite our many early mistakes, the Lord remained ever faithful. Since the time of our first small groups, DOVE Christian Fellowship International has grown into an international network of churches meeting in more than 150 congregations and a multitude of small groups throughout the United States and

Canada, Central and South America, the Caribbean, Europe, Africa, Asia and the South Pacific.[2]

The Kind of People God Calls to Leadership

Are you thinking of leading a small group? Please don't worry if you cannot see yourself as a super Christian or a great leader. Let's take a look at the kind of people God calls into leadership. This may surprise you!

- *Moses:* When God called Moses to lead the Israelites out of Egypt, Moses felt inadequate. Most leaders feel this way when the Lord calls them to any type of leadership. The first time I was ever asked to pray publicly, I read my prayer from a script I had written earlier. I was scared to death because I had not prayed in public before! The first small group I led seemed like a monumental task because I did not see myself as a born leader. But I took a step of faith.

- *Joshua, Gideon and Jeremiah:* The Lord had to encourage Joshua continually in his new role as a leader. We do not depend on our ability but upon God's ability in us! Gideon also struggled with the Lord's call to leadership in His life. Jeremiah felt the way a younger leader often feels when he or she begins to lead a small group. He thought he didn't have anything to say because he was too young. But the Lord told him not to say he was too young and not to be afraid of people. God would give him the words to say (see Jer. 1:6-8).

- *Esther:* She was an unlikely leader. She was born into poverty and was an orphan as well. But she rose from obscurity to the courts of the king and became queen over one of the most powerful empires in history. She faced difficult choices there, but she never lost her faith in God. Esther realized that everything that happened in her life prepared her for the moment she would stand before the king and plead to save her people. Hers is a story of courage and a willingness to follow God, no matter what.

These men and women felt a profound sense of inadequacy when the Lord called them to leadership, but this is the type of individual the Lord uses—someone who is completely dependent on Him! According to the Bible, God delights in manifesting His strength through our weakness (see 2 Cor. 12:9). I believe there is such a thing as a healthy sense of inadequacy.

We must be convinced that if God doesn't show up, it's all over! So, if you feel like you may be called to small-group leadership, but you don't think you have all the natural gifts you need, or you feel that you have made too many mistakes, be encouraged—you are in good company!

Questions for Discussion

1. How does change give us the opportunity to trust God more fully within the small group?

2. What is the most appealing aspect of the underground church, or small group, to you?

3. Give an example of how you have experienced community in your small group. If you have experienced a small group that did not seem to enjoy a sense of community, what was missing from the group?

Notes

1. Jesus taught that new wine needs new wineskins, because old, brittle wineskins will burst with the fermentation of new wine (see Luke 5:37).
2. For more about small groups and house churches, read my book *House to House: Growing Healthy Small Groups and House Churches in the 21st Century* (Shippensburg, PA: Destiny Image Publishers, 2009).

CHAPTER 2

A BIBLICAL VISION FOR SMALL GROUPS

*The New Testament Church Experienced
Small-Group Dynamics Every Day*

You and I were created by God to be ministers to others. Apart from this, we lack a sense of fulfillment. A small-group leader is simply a believer in Jesus Christ who makes the decision to become a minister to a small group of believers and nonbelievers.

Years ago, my journalist friend Ibrahim, from Nairobi, Kenya, had a keen interest in small groups and sought a working model to take back to his country. He asked me if he could tag along as I served in our new church made up of small groups.

He knew that our church was birthed a few years earlier with three small groups. He heard that during those times we had reminded each person, "The Bible says you are a minister, and God desires to use you!" Eventually, faith rose in their hearts, the Lord used them and new believers came to the small groups. Relationships were built. New leaders were trained.

Ibrahim watched and listened as I spent much of my time meeting with our team of pastors who were coaching our small-group leaders and discussing the needs and potential in individual members. We spoke simple, faith-filled prayers for each small-group leader and many of the believers in each small group.

One day, I saw my African brother start to weep. He unburdened his heart to me, saying, "Western evangelists come to my nation and hold massive crusades. The TV cameras are rolling. When the evangelist asks my African brothers to raise their hands to receive Christ, many respond. The next week, another Western evangelist comes to town, and many of my same brothers come to the crusade and raise their hands again. My people need a sense of fulfillment, where every individual believer understands that he is important to God and to His purposes. Will you come and help us? We need a new model of church life."

Today, Ibrahim's vision to train leaders to start small groups throughout Africa has multiplied into more than 80 congregations with hundreds of small groups scattered throughout Kenya, Uganda and Rwanda. People have received the Lord and have found a spiritual family. Ibrahim's people have received a new sense of dignity and fulfillment!

In New Zealand, where I was asked to share the vision of New Testament small-group ministry, I met Robert. He listened intently as I spoke about Jesus spending most of His time with the 12 disciples—His small group. I discussed God's call on every one of God's people to be a minister as stated in Ephesians 4:11-12. I read about the church in Acts 2 that reflected the New Testament model for effective small-group ministry. After 30 minutes, Robert spoke, filled with emotion, "When I was 13 years old, the Lord called me to be a minister. For more than 20 years, I tried to find doors that would open for me to fulfill this call. I attempted to be a minister, because I knew the Lord had called me. And as I understood it, the only way to be a minister was to be ordained after completing years of theological training. Sometime back I led a man to the Lord. I discipled him and watched him grow. It was so fulfilling. I realize tonight that I *am* a minister!" How refreshing this story has become to me as it is often repeated around the world.

Today's church has tried to reach people for Christ in our communities with extravagant church programs and twenty-first-century methodology. While such methods have their place, they can never be a substitute for personal relationships formed in the context of genuine Christian community like the early church demonstrated when they met in small groups.

God said, "Let Us make man in Our image" (Gen. 1:26, *NKJV*). The Father, Son and Holy Spirit have always experienced relationship. They are one. Shouldn't we experience the same in the church? God created Adam with the need for relationship; He said it was not good for him to be alone (see Gen. 2:18). Adam saw his need for relationship. Relationship is an established life pattern. In the church, leadership is a function put in place to help us flow together as God's people.

Even from the earliest of biblical times, God worked through spiritual family relationships. In Exodus 18:13-26, Moses receives advice from Jethro to release God's people into accountability groups to empower people to minister. He indicated there should be groups of thousands, hundreds, fifties and tens. From the very beginning, God had a plan to ease the load for leaders and keep them from burning out.

When God established His own people on the earth, He established them in tribes, clans and families. This was to ensure that every human being had a connection—an identity and relationship. The Hebrews' thought patterns were relational in nature. They thought along the lines of realizing they were in relationship because of *who* they knew. Our Greek thought or Western worldview is more information-based. Western thought says we are brought into relationship because of *what* we know. The "Jesus model" of relationship with mankind is based upon *who* you know (Jesus), not *what* you know about Him.

Jesus Set the Stage for Small Groups

Jesus ministered to the multitudes, but He spent most of His time with 12 men, His disciples. He set the stage for small-group ministry where everyone has the opportunity to get involved and begin to use his or her spiritual gifts. And even though He called 12, He gave priority to a small group of three: Peter, James and John. The small group is the place where God's people can receive training, instruction and encouragement as they reach out to their friends and neighbors with the Good News of Jesus Christ.

The Lord commands us to follow His example. Whatever He has taught us, we are to give away and teach to others. This can be quite effective through small-group ministry. For example, as a small-group leader, the most helpful way for you to teach a young husband how to love and honor his wife is for you to love and honor your wife. He sees your example. The best way to teach another Christian how to have a clear financial budget is for you to show that individual how you have set up a budget. If you believe the Lord has called you to teach a new Christian to pray, take time to pray with her! We teach others by modeling biblical truths with our own lives.

True Christianity in its simplistic form includes three focuses: (1) knowing Jesus intimately, (2) making disciples, and (3) reaching out in compassion to those who do not yet know Christ. Jesus told us to love the Lord our God with all of our heart, mind, soul and strength and to love our neighbor as ourselves (see Matt. 22:37-39). This must be the motivation of our hearts in order to effectively fulfill the Lord's purposes for us as believers in Jesus Christ. Small groups are an ideal setting for fulfilling these purposes of God.

The "House to House" Principle

In Acts 20:20, the apostle Paul declares to members of the church at Ephesus, "I kept back nothing that was helpful, but proclaimed it to you, and taught you publicly and from house to house" (*NKJV*). The early church followed Jesus' pattern of discipleship and spiritual family life. They broke bread from house to house and had larger corporate meetings.

> All the believers devoted themselves to the apostles' teaching, and to fellowship, and to sharing in meals (including the Lord's Supper), and to prayer. A deep sense of awe came over them all, and the apostles performed many miraculous signs and wonders. And all the believers met together in one place and

shared everything they had. They sold their
property and possessions and shared the
money with those in need. They worshiped together at the Temple each day, met in homes
for the Lord's Supper, and shared their meals
with great joy and generosity—all the while
praising God and enjoying the goodwill of all
the people. And each day the Lord added to
their fellowship those who were being saved
(Acts 2:42-47).

God's people gathered at the temple and met in
small groups in homes. They followed Jesus' pattern
of discipleship and spiritual family life. They broke
bread from house to house and had larger corporate
meetings. They began to minister to one another and
to pre-Christians on an individual basis, and the Lord
kept adding to the church daily!

Acts 2:42-47 gives the keys for healthy church growth:
They devoted themselves to the apostles' teaching; they
experienced fellowship by eating together; they strengthened their relationships by praying together; they lived
a lifestyle of generosity; they lived in unity with each
other; they practiced the joy of simplicity. And it happened in homes!

Peter met at Cornelius's house with his family and
friends. There was a very natural flow of evangelism that
took place as Cornelius invited those with whom he was
in relationship to hear all that Peter had to say (see Acts
10:22-48).

Some of the early church met in the house of Mary,
John Mark's mother, and experienced small-group life
as they prayed together (see Acts 12:12). The believers in

Philippi met in homes—Lydia's, for example (see Acts 16:30-34; Acts 16:15,40).

The letter that Paul wrote to the Christians in Rome was written to believers in Jesus Christ who met in peoples' homes. In his letter to the Romans, Paul indicates that one of these groups met in the home of Priscilla and Aquila: "Give my greetings to Priscilla and Aquila, my co-workers in the ministry of Christ Jesus. In fact, they once risked their lives for me. I am thankful to them, and so are all the Gentile churches. Also give my greetings to the church that meets in their home" (Rom. 16:3-5).

Paul also sent his greetings to the household of Aristobulus and the household of Narcissus (see Rom. 16:10-11). When Paul wrote to his friend Philemon, he expressed his greetings to the church in his house "and to our sister Apphia, and to our fellow soldier Archippus, and to the church that meets in your house" (Philem. 1:2). It is quite evident that the early church met in small groups in homes. And much of the entire known world was evangelized and discipled in small groups in homes within a few short years after Christ's death and resurrection.

According to church history, it was in A.D. 323, almost 300 years after the birth of the church, when Christians first met in a church building. We probably should ask ourselves this question: Has our focus on buildings and church programs caused us to lose the simplicity and the power experienced by the New Testament church?

Around A.D. 312, Constantine, the emperor of Rome, greatly influenced how Christianity was perceived when his conversion to Christianity legitimized Christianity.

Where once it was risky and life threatening to be a Christian, now it became the in thing to do, and Christians could profess their faith without fearing persecution. Everyone seemed to want to "come to Christ." The structure shifted to accommodate this change.

Before this, the spiritual life of Christians drawing from the Spirit in each other was the spark that motivated Christianity. When Christianity was widely accepted, the relational aspects of church life faltered. In its place was the new notion that all could be a part of the in crowd by joining an organization.

The small-group lifestyle and power of ministry that was taking place in people's homes and being multiplied across the earth was replaced by respectable groups that met in edifices dedicated to the glory of God. In effect, ministry was taken out of the hands of the average believer and placed in the hands of the state-sanctioned leaders. A few elite church leaders now led the masses.

In light of this, down through the ages, the church more or less lost the New Testament component of meeting in small groups and placed more of an emphasis on the church as it meets in large buildings. Although "temple ministry" is beneficial for corporate worship, teaching and celebration, perhaps the Lord wants us to get back to seeing the church as people, not as a place where believers meet. Our homes, places of business, schools and other circles of contact provide excellent places for the church to also meet in smaller groups as we infiltrate our spheres of influence with the gospel of Jesus Christ. I am convinced that the Holy Spirit has been trying to get ministry back into the hands of average believers ever since.[1]

I believe God wants to build His church through New Testament discipling (or mentoring) relationships. The Bible calls us "living stones" in 1 Peter 2:5. Each believer has been made alive through faith in our Lord Jesus Christ. The Lord builds us together with other Christians into a type of spiritual house or community.

Each living stone can only touch a small group of other believers at one time. These believers can be knit together in small groups through relationships. Ten people who are of one mind and heart can have a tremendous impact on the kingdom of darkness. The devil would like to get us alone, to isolate us, leaving us without the support of our brothers and sisters in Christ.

In small groups, we can interact meaningfully with a few other people through encouragement, prayer and practical service. As each small group obeys our Lord Jesus, the entire church will have a powerful effect on our communities as we minister together with the "living stones" the Lord has placed in our lives.

Questions for Discussion

1. Explain how Jesus set the stage for small groups.

2. Are there ways in which the church, over the past 1,700 years, has lost sight of practical Christianity? Explain your answer.

3. How has our focus on buildings and church programs caused us to lose the simplicity and the power experienced by the New Testament church?

Note
1. For more about small groups in history, read Peter Bunton, *Cell Groups and House Churches: What History Teaches Us* (Lititz, PA: House to House Publications, 2001).

AM I QUALIFIED TO BE A SMALL-GROUP LEADER?

The Primary Requirement Is to Follow Jesus' Model of Servant Leadership

In chapter 1, we mentioned that most leaders do not feel qualified to lead a small group. I felt completely unqualified when I led my first small group, but then I learned a key to leadership: According to Jesus, a leader is simply a servant! This is the first qualification for small-group leadership.

Servant Leadership

Jesus is our role model for leadership. He was and is the greatest leader who ever lived. He led by being a servant to all of those around Him. He knew who He was because of His intimate relationship with His Father, and out of that relationship He ministered to the needs of individuals. He was secure, and He was free to serve as a leader—a servant-leader. Matthew 20:25-28 indicates that the disciples had been influenced by the leadership patterns of the Gentiles. Jesus, however, explained to them that leadership in the kingdom of God is servanthood!

An attitude of serving is the key to servant leadership when leading a small group. In Matthew 25:40, Jesus says that whatever we do for one of the least of His brothers or sisters, we do for Him. In Matthew 9:36 we see the Lord's compassion for the crowds. His attitude was always to serve. Leadership must have the same heart attitude to serve.

A true Christian leader is a servant and has an intimate relationship with the Father; he or she is a person of prayer and walks in humility, being totally dependent on Jesus. If you observe a true leader when he or she is not in the spotlight, you would find that leader serving others.

I am a people watcher. I find that true leaders serve wherever they find an opportunity. There are countless ways we can serve others in a small group. You are modeling servanthood by being willing to lead a small group or assist a small-group leader. Obviously, you can't serve everyone in the world. You certainly cannot meet all the needs in a small group, but you can set the standard.

You can serve by helping someone move to a new house, by serving a meal, visiting a shut-in or praying with someone who has a need. There are hundreds of examples I could give of the servanthood that takes place within small groups. One small group gave time and money so a single mom, worn out by the demands of her young children, could take a vacation. Others have given time freely to help remodel or repaint a room in a small-group member's house or to repair a car. When a member of a small group announced that her toilet had just broken apart, with water gushing everywhere, the small group converged on her house and assisted her husband in buying and installing a new toilet. Sometimes, we must strip away our selfishness in order to serve others. In a small-group setting, we learn how to serve and to be served.

The Motivation of a Servant Leader

The number-one motivation of a servant-leader is to love God and serve His people out of a heart of love. If your primary motivation is to have a prosperous, wonderful small group, then your leadership will be misguided. Your first motivation must be to love and serve Jesus, love and serve His people and love and serve those who do not yet know Jesus. When you do this, the natural result will be a prosperous, healthy, exciting small group.

Your motivation as a small-group leader will certainly be tested at times. God may bring people into your small group who are hard for you to love. One night a young man stopped by our home. He had been a part of a Bible study that I had led. But he was backslidden and had been drinking, and he vomited all over himself in the driveway in front of our home. We took him into our home, loved him and helped him through this situation. God had given us an opportunity to practice the principles of the kingdom of God with proper motivation. We were learning how to serve.

Leaders Have a Clear Testimony

As a small-group leader, you must have a clear testimony about your salvation and your daily walk with the Lord. Areas of encounters you have had with the Holy Spirit, and healing and deliverance that you have personally experienced, should also be part of your testimony. Paul was clearly convinced about his story, saying, "For I know the one in whom I trust, and I am sure that he is able to guard what I have entrusted to him until the day of his return" (2 Tim. 1:12).

Tell your story to your small group with a sense of expectancy that God will use it to build faith in His people. Not only will it build faith, but also often God's Spirit will move, and people will be bound together in a special way after candid testimonies are shared. After one small-group leader shared his testimony, a woman who was new to the group, and sensing God's compassion and love in the room, broke down and sobbed as she revealed the pain of giving up her child for adoption as a young pregnant teenager. The small-group members were able to put their arms around her as God healed those emotions she had buried deep inside for years. It all started with a small-group leader simply sharing freely how God had saved, healed and delivered him of hurts in the past.

Leaders should also be able to regularly share how God is continuously working in their lives. They should have a testimony that is current because of the vital relationship they have with Jesus Christ.

Filled with Faith

Small-group leaders are people who are filled with faith and full of the Holy Spirit. Stephen was known as a man with these qualities (see Acts 6:5). Faith comes by hearing the Word of God, so we need to be people who love the Word of God.

As a small-group leader, you will need to exercise your faith by using the gifts the Lord has given you. How can a leader help someone else experience spiritual gifts if she does not exercise those gifts herself? For example, if the leader is not hospitable, many times the people in the small group will not learn the importance of hospitality. If the leader doesn't share his experience about being filled with the Holy Spirit, the believers in the group will not think it is very important to be filled with the Holy Spirit.

We speak what we know, but we impart who we are. If you find yourself lacking in some of these areas, talk to your local pastor or another confidant. That person can lead you to someone who has a special anointing in the area you are lacking. An anointing is the overflowing life of Jesus that imparts supernatural strength to a person in a particular area.

I've heard it said that anointing comes by association. Associate yourself with individuals God uses. Samuel received his anointing with the association of Eli the priest. The 12 disciples received from their association with our Lord Jesus Christ. And Timothy received from his mentor, Paul the apostle. Spend time with a person who has the particular anointing you desire to grow in, and expect the Lord to use you in the same way. That's what faith is all about.

Giving Encouragement

Hebrews 3:13 tells us to encourage one another daily. This is another qualification for a small-group leader—a willingness to encourage others. We can all encourage someone else; and when we sow encouragement, we will

eventually reap what we sow! This happens often outside the actual small-group meeting. Even a text message
of encouragement to someone in your small group can
make all the difference for them. Everyone gets discouraged at times. Everyone needs a friend who truly cares,
who will listen and understand him or her. And relationships take time to build.

A true leader has a servant's heart and is willing to
take the time needed to be knit with the people in his
small group. Just as it takes several weeks for a broken
bone to heal and knit together, so too it takes time for
relationships in the group to be knit together. The church
is built together through relationships: "From whom the
whole body, joined and knit together by what every joint
supplies, according to the effective working by which
every part does its share, causes growth of the body for
the edifying of itself in love" (Eph. 4:16, *NKJV*).

New Christians especially need regular encouragement and nurturing because they are like new plants in
a greenhouse. Hebrews 5:14 tells us that we grow into
maturity by practicing and training ourselves to know
the difference between right and wrong. Maturity does
not happen overnight.

A Willingness to Pray for Others

The greatest way we can serve our small group is through
prayer and giving regular encouragement. Your responsibility as a small-group leader is not to hear from
God for other people, but rather, you are called to pray
for them so that they can hear God's voice for themselves.[1] You train and build them up by praying for
them and modeling your dependency on the Word of

God. You can be a godly example as you care for and love them. They will soon be built up to hear from God for themselves about decisions they need to make in their daily lives.

A Leader Is Personable and Easy to Approach

Small-group leaders must learn to be "people oriented." A leader's attitude should be, "I will lay down my life to see the believers in our group become men and women of God." Matthew Henry, in his famous commentary on the Bible, says, "Those whose business it is to instruct people in the affairs of their souls should be humble, mild, and easy of access."[2]

A good leader cannot think, *I'll lead the meeting and teach the Bible, but I don't want to be bothered during the week with anyone's problems.* If that's the leader's attitude, that group is destined to die. Leaders must always be of the attitude, "I'm here to help!" They must be accessible. Of course, as a leader, you are not called to do everything. Learn to delegate. People learn best by doing. A small-group leader's goal should be to work himself/herself out of a job, as others' talents and gifts are multiplied.

Leaders Are Enthusiastic

It is vitally important that you genuinely care for the people in your small group and are enthusiastic about serving them. Your enthusiasm to serve Jesus and others will rub off on those in your group.

I have heard Pastor Cho from Seoul, Korea, who pastors the world's largest church of more than 800,000 people, say that the first qualification of a small-group leader is to be enthusiastic about the things of God. Enthusiasm is contagious. People want to follow someone who leads energetically. They will sense that God's work is important to you when they see you putting your whole heart into it.

Leaders Have a Gift to Lead People

Where do hurting sheep go? They go to a shepherd. Just as sheep follow shepherds, people are naturally drawn to those in the church who have a genuine gift of leadership. As a leader, God will supply you with all the grace and gifting you will need to carry out what He has called you to do.

Small-group leaders need to be constantly on the lookout for others in their group with a gift of leadership. If you notice that people are attracted to Sarah because she genuinely cares about them and serves them faithfully, encourage those leadership qualities in Sarah. Ask the Lord if He may be instructing you to ask Sarah if she would pray about being an assistant leader of your group or a part of your core team (more about this in chapter 4). God may eventually call her to lead a small group after she receives on-the-job training.

Leaders Support the Vision of the Local Church

If your small group is a ministry of your local church, you need to support the vision of your church. All families do things differently, and you must be convinced that the vision of your church is one you can embrace as your own so you can enthusiastically carry out your part in its fulfillment. Even so, there are probably no two believers on the face of the earth who agree about everything.

So then, a small-group leader in a local church is actually an extension of the leadership of the pastor and the other spiritual leaders in the church. God will command blessing when we dwell together in unity (see Ps. 133). Paul told the Corinthians in 1 Corinthians 1:10-11, "I appeal to you, brothers, in the name of our Lord Jesus Christ, that all of you agree with one another so that there may be no divisions among you and that you may be perfectly united in mind and thought" (*NIV*).

The true test of any relationship is, "What do we do when the pressure is on?" Can we stay put under fire or when we have disagreements? Unity is really a decision to "be one." It comes from the perspective of thinking "we are one" versus "we need to agree to be one."

Most people think in terms of working out a problem with another person in order to have unity. But when you make Jesus the Lord of your life, the Bible teaches that you become one with Him and also with every other believer. So when you understand Ephesians 4:3, which says, "Make every effort to keep the unity of the Spirit through the bond of peace" (*NIV*), you realize that you are in unity already; that is why you can work through the problems in order to maintain what is already there.

In wartime, nations put aside their differences to fight the bigger enemy. We have seen this enacted with the tragic terrorist events of September 11, 2001, in the United States. If nations that disagree on major things can lay aside their differences, how much more should people in the church lay aside their pet doctrines and minor differences to fight the larger enemy! When we are in settings where unity is threatened, we must ask ourselves this question: Are we really trying to help others grow in their relationship with Jesus Christ, or are we just trying to get them to see things our way?

Jesus prayed in John 17:21-23 that we would be one just as the Father and He are one. Jesus' prayer was for us to be in unity with one another.

The blessing the Lord commands over those who choose to walk in unity is life. The blessings of life in God will be poured out on small groups and churches as they walk in unity.

If there is any aspect of the ministry of the church that you, as a small-group leader, cannot consent to or support in faith, you should share your heart with your local leadership. You need to appeal to those over you in the Lord when you are having difficulty with an area in your life or in the life of the church. Many times the Lord will use your appeal to authority to bring change in an area of the church that needs modification.

Just because your opinion differs with another persons over a certain situation does not mean you are rebellious or that you cannot remain loyal. God wants you to pray about the difference of understanding you have and then talk about it with the appropriate leadership He has placed in your life.

I've been thankful for the many times when believers in the church have shared areas in which they thought we should change as a church. Some of these ideas were implemented and brought great blessing to our family of churches. It is much easier for a person in authority to receive input from one who has prayed and has a teachable spirit. It is spiritually healthy for us to appeal to the authorities that God has placed in our lives.

Leaders Are Accountable

The word "accountability" literally means *to give an account*. In our own individual lives, we are accountable to the Lord for how we live out our commitment to Christ. Our lives need to line up with the Word of God. Personal accountability is not having others tell us what to do. Personal accountability is finding out from God what He wants us to do and then asking others to hold us accountable to those things.

Years ago, I asked one of the men in our small group to hold me accountable with my personal time in prayer and in meditating on God's Word each day. Every morning at 7:00 A.M., I received a phone call as my friend checked up on me. Accountability enabled me to be victorious.

Sometimes we are held accountable for responsibilities that have been delegated to us by others whom the Lord has placed over us. For instance, employees are held accountable by their employers. In the New Testament, the apostle Paul held accountable those churches whose foundations he had labored to establish to continue to build on Jesus Christ. Paul expected the leaders of these churches to give an account to him and to the Lord for the way they were living their lives. Since the small-group leader is an extension of the leadership of the local church, the small-group leader is accountable to the local church or ministry leadership the Lord has placed in his church.

Leaders Are Facilitators

The small-group leader should primarily be a facilitator rather than the person who is doing everything. Perhaps you could write down the different roles and responsibilities needed for the group to function effectively. Then ask each member to pray about how their gifts might be used in carrying out these various areas of responsibility. This applies to the group meetings as well as relating to group members outside the meeting.

As a small-group leader, you may not be able to personally encourage everybody on a daily basis, but you can be a catalyst to encourage development of relationships within the small group. That way everyone in your group will be encouraged regularly by one another. Invite people into your home outside the meeting, or meet at Starbucks or another coffee place with two or three different people you feel might develop a relationship. See what God does. A few months ago, a young single man in our small group was looking for some mentoring, so I encouraged him to talk to two other married men in our group that I knew had wisdom from the Lord that he needed. I also encouraged both of them to pray about being spiritual fathers to him. God connected these three men in a relationship. Today he calls these two men his "spiritual fathers." Recently he was married and his spiritual fathers were both at his wedding.

A Leader Should Not Be a Novice

A new Christian should not be a small-group leader, much in the same way a three-year-old child cannot be a baby-sitter. Before a new convert to Christianity can be a leader, he needs time and experience before being entrusted with taking care of others. The Bible confirms this in 1 Timothy 3:6: "Not a novice, lest being puffed up with pride he fall into the same condemnation as the devil" (*NKJV*).

We have biblical examples: Elisha was trained by Elijah; Timothy was trained by Paul. In each case, the training took a reasonable amount of time. In the business world, workers and executives alike receive training before assuming responsibility. In the church, local leadership is responsible to discern when someone is trained and ready to lead. Each case will be different.

One possibility for new Christians who want to serve in leadership is to have them start as assistants or serve on the core team. In this role they are essentially leaders in training. Within the small group they can get the practical hands-on training they'll need to help them grow into leadership.

When an assistant leader is learning during this apprenticeship period, he or she must be allowed to fail. Small-group leaders must remember that they, too, made mistakes as they progressed through the learning process. If they remember what they went through as they matured, they will not be tempted to adopt unreasonable expectations for the leaders who come after them. A small-group leader's goal should be to support his assistants in success and failure alike and to continue to train them in love.

You may have noticed that you do not need to be a great Bible teacher to be an effective small-group leader. I will take an entire chapter later in the book to give you pointers on how to teach, but being a servant and a facilitator is much more important than being a gifted Bible teacher. In fact, during the past 40 years, I have found that the best small-group leaders are usually not gifted Bible teachers but instead lovers of people.

Questions for Discussion

1. How is an attitude of serving the key to leadership when leading a small group?

2. How have you laid down your life to see the believers in your group become men and women of God?

3. How are you training others in your small group?

Notes
1. For more on hearing God's voice, read my book *Speak Lord! I'm Listening* (Ventura, CA: Regal Books, 2008).
2. Matthew Henry, *Matthew Henry's Commentary on the Whole Bible.* http://biblecommenter.com/john/1-40.htm (accessed August 19, 2009).

CHAPTER 4

THE RESPONSIBILITIES OF A SMALL-GROUP LEADER

Practical Biblical Keys for Leading a Thriving Small Group

Small groups come in many shapes and sizes, and since each group is different, the responsibilities of the leader will vary according to the vision for the small group. However, most small groups do have some common denominators. For example, small groups are most effective when groups become a spiritual family and the leader takes on the role of a spiritual parent. As a spiritual parent, a healthy small-group leader will do all he/she can to create an atmosphere where the members in the group begin to know God better, experience community, learn how to reach those who do not yet know Jesus and make disciples. This may sound like an enormous task, but it really starts with prayer. And we know that with God, nothing is impossible!

Prayer: The First Priority

In accepting the responsibility to serve a small group, your first priority is to pray for those in the group. God has called you to "stand in the gap" (Ezek. 22:30, *NKJV*) and pray for the members. You should cover each person in prayer. Assistant leaders and core team members can assist you in being sure that everyone in your small group is covered in prayer daily. You can also pray specifically for family members, friends, and acquaintances of those in your small group who do not know Jesus. Paul said he felt as if he was going through labor pains as he prayed for the believers to grow up spiritually (see Gal. 4:19).

Praying is hard work. But one of the greatest ways to serve those within your small group is to labor in prayer for them. Ask God for direction and He will show you how to pray diligently for each person.

Praying the Scriptures has been a helpful way for me to pray. When you pray the Word of God, you can know that you are praying the Lord's will. You pray the Word by personalizing Scripture with the names of those for whom you are praying. For example, "I pray that [Brian's] love will overflow more and more, and that [Brian] will keep on growing in knowledge and understanding" (Phil. 1:9). Other excellent Scripture prayers to use in praying for spiritual growth among your group members can be found in Colossians 1:9-12, Ephesians 1:15-21 and Ephesians 3:14-19. When I pray each day for specific persons in my small group, I often pray through 12 "rooms of prayer" using the pattern found in the Lord's Prayer that Jesus used to teach His disciples to pray (see Matt. 6:9-13). If you are interested in knowing more, you can read about the 12 rooms of prayer in my book *Building Your Personal House of Prayer*.[1]

I could give countless illustrations of times when small-group members have agreed together in prayer for someone, and God has drawn that person to Himself. I like to tell the story of two new Christians, Jim and Julie, who began to pray with their small group for the salvation of Jim's father. For years, this man had been angered by any mention of God or religion, but after this group began to pray, Jim noticed that his father began to show an inquisitive attitude toward God. Jim knew the prayers of the saints were not going unnoticed. Then Jim's dad had a terrible accident. In the last hours of his life, while he was still conscious and in a clear-minded state, a nun at the hospital led Jim's dad to Jesus. Although it was difficult to see a loved one die, Jim and Julie were able to rejoice along with their small group because they knew that the prayers of small-group members had played a part in bringing Jim's dad out of the kingdom of darkness and into the kingdom of light.

As a leader, you must set the standard in prayer. Pray with your assistant leader or leaders on a regular basis. This will help alert you both to any problems that may accompany the spiritual growth that is occurring in your group. Some small groups may find it helpful for each person in the group to have a prayer partner. This may be changed periodically. Prayer teams for spiritual warfare are also effective. Small-group prayer is important because it helps us know the heart of the others in the group, which fosters spiritual intimacy and strengthens relationships. Remember to pray with expectancy! Through doubt and unbelief, the enemy will try to break our communication line to God.

If your group seems to be lacking in the area of prayer, have someone come into your group who has an anointing in the area of prayer. Prayer is contagious. As you pray with someone who has a heart and commitment to pray, your entire group will begin to experience power in prayer. Praying together will also help bring unity to the group.

Leaders Are Called to Encourage, Not to Control

One of the lessons we can learn from history is that small-group leaders who are immature or insecure may seek to control God's people rather than encourage them to hear from the Lord for themselves. Our goal must be to present every believer mature in Christ (see Col. 1:28).

We need to help the believers in our group learn how to receive direction from the Lord themselves, not encourage them to depend on us to tell them what to do.

For example, in considering questions of family finances, family size, child-rearing styles, political differences, decisions about standard of living, and so on, a small-group leader can give counsel based on his understanding of the Word of God; but these are issues not clearly decided by Scripture and ultimately must be left to the conscience of each believer. A small-group leader cannot assume the guiding role of the Holy Spirit in the life of another believer. Every believer must hear from God for himself or herself.

Leaders Should Build a Core Team

As a small-group leader, you should always keep your eyes open for those who can share the responsibility with you for leadership to help you serve the small group. This core team will include those within your small group who have enough maturity to help you plan meetings and maintain the spiritual health of the group.

People will take ownership with you for the small group when they are involved with you in praying for the small-group members and in helping to plan. The small group where my wife and I currently serve has a core team of seven who meet monthly to pray, listen to God and plan for the next month or so of the small-group meetings and discuss practical discipleship for members of the group.

My friend Randall Neighbour, in his book *The Naked Truth About Small-Group Ministry*, says, "The concept behind this model is frightfully simple; involve every willing member in the planning and execution of those plans for prayer, evangelism, fellowship, servant-hood, and meeting-related roles. Instead of the leader carrying the load, a core team of members in the group share responsibilities as co-leaders."[2]

Remember, we are not just talking about the small-group meeting! The core team can help with discipleship and the general health of the small-group spiritual family. You only need to meet with them one time each month or so for this to work. And these core team members become your top priority disciples. If they are spiritually healthy, you will probably find that the entire group is healthy.

Leaders Should Train an Assistant Leader

Jesus had a small group of 12, but He seemed to have a core team of three (Peter, James and John), and John seemed to be his closest assistant. The first qualities to look for in an assistant are those of faithfulness, humility and the willingness to serve. The best training is still the one-on-one training that takes place when a potential leader is mentored by his small-group leader. Take potential leaders along with you when you go into someone's home to pray for them. It has always been a joy for me to lead others to Christ as another believer joins with me as an apprentice and a prayer partner. This way he can witness the miracle of a new birth. Jesus set the pattern for on-the-job training. He spent most of His time training a few men, not teaching great crowds.

My friend John still talks about the times when he joined me to witness to people in a local park. We walked through the park and took a step of faith in obedience to the Lord as He led us to share the gospel with certain individuals. This was a life-changing experience for John.

Throughout the years, we have found that there are two basic types of assistant leaders and core team members who serve alongside the leader: (1) those being developed for future small-group leadership, and (2) those who are called to remain assistants. Here is a brief definition for each type of assistant leader:

1. Someone being trained for future small-group leadership—this person will begin to take on the responsibility with you for various areas of leadership in your small group and will eventually either start a new small group, or you may turn the leadership of the present small group over to this person.

2. Someone who is not a potential small-group leader is an assistant leader; however, when

a small group multiplies, this person gives a sense of stability and continuity to one of the new groups. He may always serve in a supportive role and not ever be called to be a small-group leader.

Set the Example

You can set the example by sharing your own personal needs and problems with those in your group. The Bible tells us in 2 Corinthians 12:9 that we should boast in our weaknesses so that the power of Christ may rest upon us. When we are open about areas of struggle we've had and share how the Lord has given us grace to conquer by His Word, it causes us to be transparent. This keeps us from being placed upon a pedestal. When people put us on a pedestal, we open ourselves to the enemy in the area of pride. People we are serving feel as though they can never attain our level of spirituality, which is totally untrue.

My friend Carl was leading a small group and asked the group members one evening if anyone had any difficulties they were facing that the group could pray with them about. Everyone said they were fine. Then Carl took a few minutes and shared some difficulties in his own life and asked for prayer. He told me later, "It was amazing. Within a few minutes everyone in the group had a personal prayer request!" Carl led the way by being vulnerable, and the others in the group then felt free to be open with their lives.

We can minister most effectively by showing the people in our group what the Word of God says rather than by giving them our own opinions. If you don't have the answer, don't fake it. Tell them honestly that you don't know but that you will help them find the answer.

Leaders should not give strong advice or correction to a person they do not know very well (unless they are clearly led by the Holy Spirit). Much patience is needed before attempting to correct someone's faults. Simply continue to love and care for them, and many times they will come to you for advice and help. They will see in you an example of how they themselves want to be.

True leaders will take time—all the time that is necessary—to build good, trusting relationships with people. We must build relationships not only within the setting of the group meeting, but also outside the meeting as well. Through informal time spent in social interaction outside of the meeting context, the time will eventually come when you will feel free to speak into the lives of the people in your group because of the trust that has been established. If you don't have a relationship with the people in your group, it will be very difficult for them to receive advice or correction from you.

Plan Group Social Activities and Work Projects

You should periodically initiate activities for your group to further build relationships. Sports events, community service, eating together and local evangelistic outreaches are just a few examples of the kinds of activities in which your group can participate. It is not necessary for each activity to include everyone in the group. One or two group members can get together for a baseball game or for a craft session. These can be great activities to reach those who do not know Christ.

People who are gifted in the area of organization in the small group could be assigned to help plan activities. It helps to delegate responsibility to others, because it will give people a sense of healthy stewardship for what God is doing. Remember, small groups are called to be teams, working together to build the kingdom of God.

A work project is an excellent way to bond as a small group and help someone as well. Nick recalls how his small group surprised his family with their help on some much-needed home improvements:

There's a popular show on TV called *Extreme Makeover Home Edition*. Maybe you have even shed a tear or two as the families see their new homes for the first time. Well, my wife and I now feel like we can relate. We were the recipients of an "extreme makeover" from our small group. For the past couple of years, there have been several projects around the house that have desperately needed attention, but the resources just simply weren't there. It had really become a huge burden seeing these needs on a daily basis. Our small group took notice and sent us away for a weekend. It was a huge blessing, but it was actually just a diversion to keep us out of the house while the bigger blessing was being set in motion. When we returned from our trip, we were greeted by a crowd of workers hiding out in our garage, waiting to see our reaction to their labor of love. They had replaced our roof, fixed the gutters, re-landscaped the lawn, painted the house, built a new pantry, completely remodeled our bathroom, and re-decorated our bedroom! It was simply over-whelming. The love of God and the love of our brothers and sisters is truly amazing . . . and humbling. This is love—not just spoken or written, but fully illustrated and punctuated with an exclamation mark!

Special Events

Small groups can also meet for breakfast or for a meal during a day off or over a lunch break.

Birthdays and anniversaries are an important part of our lives. Some of the believers that the Lord has placed in your group may not have a family who cares about them, or their families may live in another state. Remembering birthdays, anniversaries and other special events with cards and an occasional party can be a tremendous source of encouragement to them. Perhaps someone in the group could compile a list of birthdays and anniversaries that could be photocopied and passed out to the entire group.

A few small groups from one of our churches in Barbados held an art exhibit that raised money for orphanages in Haiti and Mexico. This charity exhibition was organized and staffed by members of the small groups and featured an artist from the group. Thousands of dollars were given toward the costs by business owners and philanthropists to make it a huge success. Some divine appointments happened during the course of the event and one man gave his heart to Jesus.

Leading the Meetings

As a small-group leader, you are responsible to lead the small-group meetings or make sure someone is leading it. Speaking of the meeting itself, in the next chapter we will look at the dynamics of leading the small-group meeting.

Questions for Discussion

1. Describe the basic job description of a small-group leader.

2. In what ways might a leader struggle with control in the small group?

3. List some ways a leader can give on-the-job training to others.

Notes
1. Larry Kreider, *Building Your Personal House of Prayer* (Shippensburg, PA: Destiny Image Publishers, 2008).
2. Randall Neighbour, *The Naked Truth About Small-Group Ministry* (Houston, TX: Touch Publications, 2009), p. 184.

CHAPTER 5

GET MAXIMUM PARTICIPATION

Healthy Dynamics of a Small-Group Meeting

I am always a bit hesitant to give guidelines for what should happen at a small-group meeting because I believe it is so easy to trust the format rather than to stay truly open to what the Holy Spirit wants you to do. But so many pastors and small-group leaders have asked me to share these guidelines that I believe I need to address this subject. So here goes.

Many times the small-group meeting includes a time of worship, testimonies, a short teaching, a time for response to the teaching, announcements, prayer and sharing of life together. The format can be changed and altered in a thousand ways. You do not have to do all of these things or, in reality, any of these things. Every time you come together, expect God to do something new among you. Do not get stuck in a rut. I once heard that a rut is a grave with the ends knocked out. Doing the same thing week after week will bring spiritual death into your group.

It is important that you follow the leading of the Holy Spirit when you conduct your meetings. Unless you are clearly led otherwise, I encourage you to keep the meeting to about an hour to no more than one-and-a-half hours in length. And always be prepared! Prayerfully make a schedule and stick to it, unless you know that the Holy Spirit is leading otherwise. Always be open to the leading of the Holy Spirit, and be willing to throw your preparations aside.

There is no excuse to say you are following the Holy Spirit if in actuality you are simply unprepared. Many times we say that we are following the Holy Spirit when in reality we have been lazy and undisciplined. This is a disgrace to our Lord and to His people. To waste people's time shows poor leadership.

Especially in new groups, it is advantageous to start the first meetings with ice-breakers of some sort. You could begin with an open-ended sentence. Here are some examples—some to chuckle over and some to provoke thought:

Lighthearted or Humorous Beginnings
"My most embarrassing moment was when . . ."
"One of the best times of my life was . . ."
"If I had a million dollars, I would . . ."
"My idea of a perfect evening is . . ."
"What I want for Christmas is . . ."
"When I am 70 years old, I want to be doing . . ."
"My favorite time of day is . . ."
"One thing I enjoy about my job (or school) is . . ."
"The fastest I ever drove is . . ."
"My favorite dessert is . . ."
"My favorite Bible verse is . . ."

More Serious Starters
"I want to praise God for . . ."
"What I'm thankful for this week is . . ."

"Someone blessed me by doing . . ."
"My toughest experience happened when . . ."
"I'm working at . . . in my life."
"Some personal vision I have for my life is . . ."

Questions to Ask on a Regular Basis to Keep Everyone Sharp

"What God is speaking personally to me is . . ."
"What I am learning from the people I am serving
with in my small group is . . ."[1]

If possible, a small group should try to have at least
one person designated to lead the group in worship. If a
person is selected for this ministry, he or she does not need
to play an instrument—although many do—but should be
able to lead in worshipful singing unto the Lord. If you do
not have a worship leader, spend time in prayer instead.
You could also make use of CDs, worship DVDs and
sound tracks that enhance the times of singing to the Lord.
Encourage the small-group members to come to the meetings with a song or a hymn to share with the others. When
everyone feels a sense of responsibility before the Lord for
what happens at the meeting, you can expect the Lord to
move through His body in a powerful way.

It is important to take some time to focus on the
Word of God during the meeting. I suggest a short teaching from Scripture for 10 to 15 or 20 minutes with lots
of time to ask questions and discuss. Some small groups
discuss the pastor's sermon from the past weekend.
If someone from your group is going to teach, give them
some guidelines to teach in a way that is not boring. I have
dedicated the entire next chapter to this subject.

Make sure that you start and stop your meetings
at the agreed-upon times, unless the Holy Spirit leads

you otherwise. Be respectful of other people's time, especially parents of babies and school children who must study.

The time following the meeting is full of opportunities for sharing and meeting the spiritual needs of the people. This is often the most important time of the meeting. Those who must leave may go, and those who want to seek help from the leader or others in the group are free to do so. Many times after the meetings, small clusters of people may gather together in various areas of the home to share heart to heart and pray together. These times of informal fellowship are invaluable as our fellow believers surround us with compassion and give us the courage to keep going so we will be able to stand tall, embodying the very fullness of Christ (see Eph. 4:11-16).

Food served at the meetings can be fun, entertaining and promote relationships. This usually adds an element of warm hospitality. However, food can also become competitive between members or an extra expense for the hosts. Don't allow food to become the focus. If snacks are regularly served at the meeting, keep them simple and allow members to share the responsibility to bring them.

Maintaining Order During the Meeting

Keep the meeting moving and alive. Whoever has been given responsibility for a particular part of the meeting must be enthusiastic about his part or the meeting will falter and be of no benefit. People will be bored.

If there are those who constantly interrupt, they should be gently confronted with the truth that they need to consider others as more important than themselves (see Phil. 2:3). In 1 Corinthians 14:26, Paul tells us, "What then shall we say, brothers? When you come together, everyone has a hymn, or a word of instruction, a revelation, a tongue or an interpretation. All of these must be done for the strengthening of the church" (*NIV*).

If you feel that your meetings are getting out of hand because one person monopolizes the time, you may need to encourage that person who is overly verbal to allow others time to share. Ask him or her to stick to a time limit.

If someone takes the meeting down a side street by getting off the subject, you can tactfully say that you will be happy to talk privately about it after the meeting. This way you can honor him or her as a person, and you can keep the meeting from becoming boring for the rest of the people.

The Leader Is Responsible to Oversee the Meetings

Delegate as much responsibility as you can to others, but remember that you are still responsible for the protection and the spiritual health of what happens at the meetings. For example, some prayer requests in a meeting should be handled outside of the meeting. If someone is struggling with a life-controlling problem or in areas that need deliverance, it may be best to pray for them after the meeting is over or at another time.

It's amazing how quickly small-group meetings become boring! Why does this happen? We stop asking the Father to renew our vision and end up doing the same old stuff every week. New traditions can crystallize quickly. When we neglect to hear a fresh word from the Father to see what He wants to do among us, small-group rigor mortis sets in. Rigor mortis is the stiffening of the body after death. If we are careless, our groups can slide into the first stages of spiritual rigor mortis. Jesus told the Pharisees that He only did what He saw the Father doing (see John 5:19). He was in constant relationship with His Father in heaven, listening to His voice.

Take Time to Pray

Remember, when we gather in His name He promises to be with us (see Matt. 18:20)! We need to acknowledge the Lord when we are together (see Prov. 3:6). Make prayer a natural part of small-group life. Acknowledge the Lord when you begin the meeting and thank Him when the meeting concludes. Spontaneously pray throughout the meeting whenever someone mentions a need. Pray for missionaries. Pray for those who need a relationship with the Lord in your families and in your communities. Make communing with God a natural part of small-group life, just like breathing is a natural part of living.

Many small groups use the concept of a "hot seat," a chair where a person in the group sits to receive prayer from their small-group family. Prayer is vital for our lives as believers in Jesus. We can model this in small-group ministry.

When you listen for specific needs as the people share, you can then pray for them as a group. Prayer should be planned as a vital part of your time together. Ask someone beforehand to open with prayer. Have a time for intercession and praise. Give everyone an opportunity to pray. Be helpful and encouraging when people are learning to pray out loud.

One of the men in a group that I led a few years back was scared to pray publicly. He knew that he had to deal with this fear. He told me to ask him to pray in front of the other men in the group when we met together to pray every other week before work in the mornings. As I asked him to pray and encouraged him, he went on to lead various groups in the years that followed. He just needed some encouragement and accountability in the group setting.

Be Creative

When I was a new small-group leader, a young couple in our group phoned me an hour before the meeting, "We can't come tonight, because we have to do lawn work."

I muttered to myself, *Isn't our group more important than their lawn work?* With a complete lack of compassion and a hefty dose of pride, I continued mumbling, *If they were committed, they'd get their priorities straight.* Then the Father got my full attention with an innovative thought. *Let's take the entire group to their home and help them!* Working together on their lawn was a blast! We followed what the Father was doing in the lives of this young couple (building a relationship with them) and the Lord honored our obedience.

One of the small groups in our city recently realized they were spending too much time focused on themselves rather than on serving hurting people in their community. So they decided to meet every other week at a local coffee shop, hang out and talk to people in the community. They are enjoying this time at the coffee shop because it is what the Father is doing among them.

A Place to Meet

Choosing the right location in which to meet is an important decision. One time, a small-group leader in our church was at his place of business, chatting with a customer. In the course of their conversation, the customer mentioned that they have difficulty parking on their street on Wednesday evenings due to the Jehovah's Witnesses who meet in a house on that street. Then the small-group leader noticed that the customer's check address was on the same street as where his group met!

Well, that group promptly decided to make cookies and give them out to each family on their block and explain who they were and what they believed. This squashed the rumor and helped build relationships with the people in their neighborhood. Additionally, they tried to carpool more, so that they didn't take up all the parking space on the block during the small-group meeting night!

Not all small groups will meet at the same location week after week. Frequently, small groups will rotate the meeting location between various group members' homes. When deciding whose home your group will meet in, here are some things to consider: Is the location central for the majority of the people in your group? Does it have a large enough room for the group to gather in with space for newcomers? If needed, is there a separate room for children's ministry? Does the home offer a comfortable and relaxing atmosphere to adults and children as well? Are the hosts relaxed about using their home or are they nervous about things being broken or ruined? Are the hosts financially able to meet the needs that hosting a group involves? This question is of special significance in cultures where serving coffee, tea and cookies or biscuits is expected.

Some small groups meet twice a month and others may meet together each week. Sometimes groups will alternate a regular meeting with an outreach or game night. Or sometimes the women will meet separately from the men in rotating weeks. The men or women may get together for breakfast or go bowling.

Tips for Including Children in the Meetings

The Lord values children. Children should take an active role in small-group life. Remember, children are the church of today! The perspectives of the parents and other adults in the group will play a major role in determining how each individual group integrates children. Here are some of the many options for you to consider.

Family Participation with Separate Children's Ministry Time

It seems that the majority of small groups in North America prefer this option. Children join their parents for the first part of the meeting and meet separately for the second part. Children are incorporated into the time of worship, testimonies and prayer. Then the children receive their own ministry in another room or place.[2]

Who ministers to the children when they meet separately? Various small-group members can take turns ministering to the children on a rotating basis. Older children can minister to younger children. Parents can take turns ministering to the children. A team can be formed using only one parent from a family so the other parent can attend the meeting. This will help keep unity and continuity in the group. At times, we have had a person from another church (or another small group that met at a different time) serve in our children's ministry. Small groups sometimes pay the children's workers if they are from another small group or another church.

Total Family Participation

In this option, children stay with their parents for the entire meeting. The teaching and worship is geared to the children, and families learn together. Gear worship time for children and let them freely participate. Have them pray for the adults. Supply the children with homemade instruments or noisemakers and allow them to express themselves in worship. You could also use a Christian children's music video and dance before the Lord like David did! For the teaching time, collect visual aids or props that will help you tell the story. Build in opportunities for the children to participate. Ask questions; create body motions or sound effects they can do as you tell the story. Remember that young children think concretely, not abstractly; they learn by doing and experiencing.

Basic Childcare

Some parents prefer to hire a baby-sitter for their younger children. This gives the parents a night out. They can receive uninterrupted ministry and learn to minister to others while their children are cared for at home. In other cases, when an outside person comes in each time to minister to the children in the small group, an offering is taken for this "baby-sitter."

Older Children Serving Younger Children

You could give each older child a turn at planning activities for the rest of the children. Supervised by the adult, the child is in charge. He or she may choose to share a Scripture that means a lot to him personally, or choose to have the rest of the children do pantomimes of Bible events and then guess what it is. The child in charge may appoint Scripture readers or persons to close in prayer. This gives children an opportunity to be creative and also exercise spiritual gifts.

Every child can be a mature Christian for his own age. Faith development is a process occurring alongside the other aspects of growth. A small group can offer children a spiritual home and family—a place to belong. In the home group, children have the opportunity to express love and gratitude to God through worship and praise. Mentoring can also take place in this safe and loving environment. Seeds are sown in children's lives that will bear fruit. Small groups can be lots of fun for children!

Caution with children: In light of the world and day we live in, we advise two childcare persons to serve together. These should be persons you know, trust and believe will give proper and safe care to your children.

Each One Brings Something

Get everyone involved. In 1 Corinthians 14:26, each one brings something to the meeting. Remember, the meeting is not a miniature church service! Everyone can participate in a small-group meeting. Call people before the meeting and ask them to share, pray, greet, and so forth. Do not do anything in the meeting that someone else can do.

Always remember that much of small-group life often happens outside the meetings. Relationships are the key! For example, when people pray together informally or one-on-one after the meeting, relationships are built that surpass those found in the "formal" meeting.

One more important truth to remember: A small-group meeting is not a social club, but a time when, together, you meet with God. The Word of God needs to be central and taught in a way that revolutionizes lives. In the next chapter we will learn practical biblical keys to teaching the Bible with great confidence.

Questions for Discussion

1. When a small-group member communicates a need to the leader, what steps can be taken to help meet the need?

2. What can the group do to minister to the children, and how can the children minister to the group?

3. How can you encourage everyone to bring something to the meeting?

Notes
  1. Karen Ruiz and Sarah Mohler, *Creative Ideas for Cell Groups* (Lititz, PA: House to House Publications, 1996).
  2. We recommend a creative learning experience for children that teaches the basics of Christianity: Jane Nicholas, *Biblical Foundations for Children* (Lititz, PA: House to House Publications, 1999).

CHAPTER 6

TEACH WITH CONFIDENCE

How to Teach the Bible to a Small Group of People Without Boring Them

The first time I stood in front of a group of people to present a teaching from the Bible, my heart was beating furiously, my knees trembled and my voice quivered. I knew that God had given me something to say, so I struggled on through, trying not to hyperventilate or sweat too much. Although I considered myself to be a fairly articulate person, I turned into a quivering mass of jelly in front of the group—and the group contained only five people!

Since that time many years ago, I have taught in small groups and large. I eventually discovered some biblical principles and practical tips that made teaching enjoyable for me.

You do not have to have the gift of being a charismatic teacher to be effective in teaching, especially in a small group. Everyone in the Body of Christ is called to impart truth. Teaching others in a small group is simply imparting truth to others.

An Effective Teacher Loves People

To be an effective teacher, you must have a genuine love for the people you teach. Love and service to people overflow out of your love for Jesus that floods your heart with caring and compassion for others. As you teach, the warmth of your unique God-given personality will flow out to the group. If God calls you to teach in a small group, you simply will be sharing your life and the truth that God has imparted to you with others. You are being obedient to help others know Him better through His Word.

When teaching is bathed in prayer, it becomes a part of our lives so that we can impart it to others. Luke 6:12 tells us how Jesus prayed: "Now it came to pass in those days that He went out to the mountain to pray, and continued all night in prayer to God" (*NKJV*).

I read once that Charles Finney, a great American evangelist living during the nineteenth century, got up at 4:00 A.M. and prayed for four hours. When he taught the Bible, people came under intense conviction. Thousands were converted under Finney's teaching.

Prayer will prepare people's hearts to receive the teaching we give so they can be changed and become more like Jesus. Be specific when you pray! Pray for each person by name, asking the Holy Spirit to open each heart to the Word of God.

When you have spent time praying, you will find that people will be drawn to you as a teacher, because the favor of God will be on you. Psalm 5:12 tells us, "For You, O LORD, will bless the righteous; with favor You will surround him as with a shield" (*NKJV*). Expect the Lord to place His favor on you as you teach His Word.

Teach the Word, Not Your Opinions

Someone once said that opinions are like the nose on your face; everyone has one! A teacher needs to teach the

Word, not merely ideas and opinions. The fact is, our opinions will never change anyone's life; only the Word of God changes lives.

Teachers need to "Preach the word! Be ready in season and out of season" (2 Tim. 4:2, *NKJV*). God's Word stands up by itself. It is powerful. Have the people you teach look up the Scriptures you are using, so they can see it for themselves. Remember, "Faith comes by hearing, and hearing by the Word of God" (Rom. 10:17, *NKJV*).

Use Visuals and Illustrations

Many people are visual learners. Mental pictures always help to focus a message and make it easier to remember. A man in the African bush once asked an American what the Empire State Building looked like. The American used a mental picture the man could relate to. He said it looked like 200 mud huts stacked on top of each other with a banana leaf sticking out of the top. To a man who had never seen a tall building, it was the closest thing he could understand. Be practical in your teaching and use illustrations people can readily understand.

Jesus constantly used parables or story illustrations that conveyed a spiritual meaning when He taught. "All these things Jesus spoke to the multitude in parables; and without a parable He did not speak to them" (Matt. 13:34, *NKJV*). Jesus knew that spiritual things are often not tangible until we "see" a natural illustration that points us to the spiritual implication. Jesus used mental pictures of a sower sowing seeds or a lost sheep or a hidden treasure. These pictures helped the people understand what He was saying. A good teacher will use stories describing current events or famous people to relate a spiritual concept to the people he is teaching.

Years ago, I read a book of sermons by D. L. Moody, the renowned evangelist of the late 1800s. I was amazed that two-thirds of the content of his sermons were illustrations. This evangelist, who led one million people to Jesus, knew the importance of using stories and illustrations to help people understand spiritual concepts.

Some of the greatest illustrations you can give as a teacher are those from your own life. When I teach on prayer, I often tell of the time my family prayed for money to pay a bill and found money scattered on our front lawn. It only happened once, but it is a powerful illustration to tell of God's supernatural ability to answer prayer. When I teach on salvation, I give my testimony. When I teach on marriage, I use examples from my own life. People love stories! It helps them remember spiritual truth.

Don't Use Christianeze!

Use plain, everyday language when you teach, not the church-y language that only seasoned Christians can understand. Words like "sanctification" and "propitiation" will not be understood by a young Christian unless you take the time to explain the words to him. A newly saved young man went to a church meeting and told me later, "That preacher used thousand-dollar words. I didn't understand a thing." The preacher was talking over the heads of the people and probably lost many in the process.

John Wesley practiced his sermons on his eight-year-old servant girl. If she understood the points he was trying to get across, he used the sermon. One day Wesley took one of his preachers-in-training to the market, where they came upon two women who were fighting and cursing each other. "Let's get out of here," said the preacher.

"No, wait a minute," said Wesley. "I want to teach you how to preach." He wanted the preacher to understand and use the language that the common people used (minus the curse words, of course!), and not the church-y language of the day (which most clergy used while preaching).

Speak the Truth in Love

Don't speak down to the people you are teaching. This often happens when a teacher preaches at his audience instead of including them as he teaches. This creates a chasm between him and the group. He is talking at them instead of to them.

A good teacher endeavors to develop a rapport between the group and himself so that the flow of communication moves smoothly between the two. He often uses words like "we" and "us" to build a relationship with his audience. He makes the group feel as if he, too, has struggled or is struggling with some of the life issues he is addressing. When a teacher speaks on the people's level, he lifts them up rather than pushing them down and discouraging them.

Teach with Enthusiasm

Did you ever sit in a Sunday School class, Bible study or other church meeting when the speaker droned on endlessly and practically put you to sleep? Although what was said concerning God's Word was true, it may have been presented like a list of facts or like a grocery list, which wouldn't hold anyone's attention.

God has called us to minister His life when we teach. It's not the words themselves that are going to cause people to listen, but how we say them. If the teaching presented is one that we believe ourselves, having received the life of Jesus in us, we will communicate this life-giving message. We will engage the group, having caught their attention, because we are excited about the message. Things that are personally important to us always come across with great impact to those we teach.

When we are totally convinced of the reality of Christ, our enthusiasm will show. An actor in London was talking with a pastor, who admitted, "I don't understand it. On Saturday night your theaters are full, and yet on Sunday mornings, we can scarcely get anyone to attend our meetings. You use fiction and move the assembly to tears. We ministers represent reality and scarcely obtain a hearing."

The actor replied, "Maybe it is because we represent fiction as reality and you represent reality as fiction!" I think the actor was correct. A teacher should not be afraid to act while he is teaching. Speaking in front of a group is different from conversational skill and takes more active mental "thinking on your feet" kind of skills involving concentration, coordination and quick response to distractions.

Did you ever watch someone teach who never moves? Your eyes start to glaze over and your mind drifts off. When a teacher moves his hands and body, it proves he is alive. He is not glued to his chair or the podium! Movement obligates the group you are teaching to keep their eyes open!

Teach in Faith

A study listing what people are most afraid of showed that speaking before a group is the most fearsome thing in life—worse than insects and bugs, flying, sickness or loneliness. If you have never taught before, it may be scary at first; but even experienced teachers get nervous—it's normal! The experienced teacher has simply learned to make use of his tension and put it to good use. For example, he may turn the nervousness into greater expressiveness.

Whenever you face a group as a teacher, you are making yourself "stick out" (the others have the anonymity of the group). That's why your nervous system is going full-throttle. People are looking at you, expecting to receive something—often hoping it will be brilliant!

Since you believe you have something worth saying and have studied and prayed and want to communicate it clearly to your listeners, your jitters will soon disappear as you gain confidence after a minute or so of teaching. It helps to pick out the friendliest and most interested face in the group and talk to him or her first. Soon you will make eye contact with more people and feel increasingly relaxed as they respond to your teaching.

The good side to nervousness is that it activates your adrenaline supply. It makes your eyes shine and animates you. It also activates the brain and helps put an edge on what you are saying. And you can depend on the fact that you are not alone. The Holy Spirit is there to help you speak His words. As you pray, the Holy Spirit replaces all fear with faith!

Speak with Authority

You have received authority from God, as a believer in Jesus Christ, to share His Word. Jesus, the most effective teacher who ever lived, spoke with authority: "On the Sabbath He entered the synagogue and taught. And they were astonished at His teaching, for He taught them as one having authority, and not as the scribes" (Mark 1:21-22, *NKJV*). Jesus amazed the people because He taught differently from the other religious leaders of His day. He knew where He got His authority, and it showed.

Not only have you received God's authority, but you have also received authority from the leaders of the church where you serve. Whenever I speak in a local church, I submit to the authority of the leadership there. In order to have authority, we need to be under authority, both God's and the church's. A policeman who holds up his hand to stop traffic has authority, which is backed up by the government. You, as a small-group teacher, have spiritual boldness and authority given to you by God and by your church leadership.

Be Prepared

Take time to prepare the teaching for the small group. A quick five-minute glance at teaching notes and a hurried prayer do not constitute preparation. Rambling words are distracting and bore people.

Over the years, I have attended many different small-group meetings and have found some teachings to be boring and others dynamic. In almost every instance, after speaking with the teacher, I discover that the key is whether or not the teacher has adequately prepared. A teacher who has prepared—who has studied his topic and prayed—will be enthusiastic and confident, and that spirit will flow out to his audience.

Good preparation of a teaching, along with complete dependence on the Holy Spirit to communicate that teaching to others, is a better understanding of "God giving us the words to say." One teacher of a small group once said, "I have my notes, but I am still free to obey God as He leads me, by the Holy Spirit, sometimes in other directions." I heartily agree.

Be Personable

Any audience, including a small group, usually reflects the attitude and manner of the teacher. Think about it. If you are a funny guy, people will be relaxed and smile at your humor. If you are stilted and nervous, the audience will be uncomfortable, holding its collective breath. And, of course, if you are boring, they will be fast asleep!

As most teachers know, if no relationship is developed between the teacher and the audience, it can hinder a vital message from being received. The Holy Spirit uses relationships to build trust between the teacher and the audience. When a teacher shares heart issues from his own life, he is no longer just communicating facts; he opens up his life and is vulnerable to those He is teaching, causing them to be more susceptible to receiving the teaching. Otherwise, people go home without their needs being met, and it turns out to be just another useless meeting.

It is important for a teacher to initially draw people in. By looking people in the eye, you connect with them, telling them they are important. Continue to focus on individuals as you speak and include their names during the teaching: "So you see, Sandy, our heavenly Father loves you so much; He calls you His child!"

I was in a small group one time and attempted, during my teaching, to include a man who had just been released from jail. As I occasionally used his name during the teaching, he felt love and caring extended to him. At the end of the evening, he took a step of faith and asked us to pray for him. God's love broke down the walls of fear and intimidation in his life.

Receive Constructive Criticism

No teacher is beyond the need for improvement. Most teachers want to know if they are using excessive hand gestures or constantly repeating the phrase "you know." After I preach or teach, I have often asked people to give me good constructive criticism so that I can grow in my ability to teach. A good teacher learns to accept criticism and profit by it. Discovering your weaknesses is the first step to correcting them.

One excellent way to personally critique yourself is by videotaping yourself while teaching. You can see yourself as your audience sees and hears you and immediately recognize your strengths and weaknesses as a speaker. This self-evaluation can be a great time to upgrade your teaching skills as you learn to correct your weaknesses and emphasize and develop your strengths.

Share this chapter on teaching with those you ask to teach in your small group. Perhaps give them the opportunity to teach a mini-message of five minutes or so the first time, so it is not too daunting for them. And then give them lots of encouragement. This is what mentors do, they get under those the Lord places in their lives and they pray for them and spend extra time with them. This is a key to healthy small-group ministry. We'll learn more about mentoring in the next chapter.

Questions for Discussion

1. Explain how a teacher can teach in faith and with authority.

2. If you don't have a gift of teaching, how can you compensate?

3. How has the Holy Spirit used relationships in your small group to build trust between the teacher and the group?

CHAPTER 7

BECOME A SPIRITUAL MOM OR DAD

The Role of Spiritual Mentors
in a Small-Group Setting

I will never forget the experience of being a natural father for the first time. I had faithfully attended prenatal classes with LaVerne, where I learned how to coach her through delivery. When the actual contractions started, reality hit me, and I hit the panic button. We were going to have a baby! (Well, okay, LaVerne was, but I was on the team.) I wasn't ready! I was too young! I wasn't experienced! I wanted to tell LaVerne, "Couldn't you just put it on hold for a few months until we are ready for this?" That was not an option. It was time, and she gave birth to a baby girl.

Twenty-two years later, I walked down the aisle with this "baby" girl at my side and gave her away to a young man to be his wife. We raised her to give her away. Now she would have the opportunity to be a parent and prepare the next generation.

Just as we raise our natural children, we must train everyone in our small groups to become spiritual parents. That is what small-group ministry is all about:

preparing and training future spiritual fathers and mothers (mentors).

Recently I spoke to a group of young people at one of America's dynamic mega churches, and a young man approached me after my session. "I'm on staff here, but I'm leaving next month," he confided.

I was puzzled. "Why?"

He said, "Larry, if just one person in leadership in this church had sat down with me for an hour once a month for a cup of coffee and asked me how I was doing, I would stay." He was looking for a spiritual mentor—someone to spend some time with him, someone who could offer support and guidance and feedback as he learned to use his gifts and talents. But everyone was too busy, and the many church programs had to go on.

Paul noticed a similar phenomenon in the Corinthian church. The believers there had many teachers in their spiritual lives, but few spiritual mentors, and they were immature as believers. "For though you might have ten thousand instructors in Christ, yet you do not have many fathers" (1 Cor. 4:15, *NKJV*). They lacked true parents or mentors to give them proper training and nurturing—to help them put their knowledge into practice.

As a small-group leader, you have the privilege to serve in the role of a spiritual father or mother to your members. To follow the pattern of Jesus who had 72 disciples, yet had 12 and also the inner circle of 3, there are levels and degrees of mentoring that can happen in small-group ministry. As a spiritual father or mother, you can be a mentor to those in your group, because you help your spiritual sons and daughters along on their spiritual journey. But you also need to pray as Jesus did to find those that you need to be spending more time with so they can in turn mentor others in your group.

So what is a spiritual father or mother? Simply stated, my favorite definition is: "A spiritual father or mother helps a spiritual son or daughter reach his or her God-given potential." That, in a nutshell, is your goal as a small-group leader!

Jesus took 12 men and became a spiritual father to them for three-and-a-half years. He knew that Kingdom values were caught more than taught. Though He ministered to the multitudes, He spent most of His time with the 12 disciples, who changed the world. The Lord expects us to do the same, and small groups provide an ideal venue in which to learn how to mentor others and be mentored ourselves.

Mom? Dad? Where Are You?

God's intention is to produce spiritual parents who are willing to nurture spiritual children and help them grow into spiritual parents. This is a fulfillment of the Lord's promise to "turn the hearts of the fathers to the children, and the hearts of the children to their fathers" (Mal. 4:6, *NKJV*). Most small groups in America seem to be missing this extremely important component in small-group ministry. Children, both natural and spiritual, need parents who nurture strong character and assure them that they are valuable—that they are gifts from God. As children mature, they in turn can nurture the next generation. The potential for spiritual mentoring is truly enormous in small groups. And much of it happens outside of the actual meeting.

You've probably heard that geese fly in a V formation because the aerodynamics of the V enable the geese to fly more than 70 percent farther than if they fly alone. As each bird flaps its wings, an updraft is created for the bird behind it. When the bird in front gets tired, it moves back in the formation. Geese go a lot farther when they work together. That is the point of a mentoring relationship—we can go a lot farther spiritually if we work together in family-like units to reach the world.

As a small-group leader, God has called you to become a spiritual father or mother. No matter what you do—whether you are a housewife, a student, a worker in a factory, a pastor of a church, a missionary, or the head a large corporation—you can become a spiritual father or mother.

Spiritual impartations are passed on practically and easily from parents to children as they are trained in the spiritual "boot camp" of small groups. I served as the pastor of a small-group-based church in Pennsylvania for 15 years, and in the process of our church growing and multiplying, hundreds of spiritual fathers and mothers were released as ministers to God's people through the small groups. Many moved on to assume roles of greater responsibility in the Lord's kingdom.

All of us are called to be spiritual fathers or mothers to someone—maybe to a "pre-Christian." Small groups are a part of God's plan to establish spiritual fathers for the harvest of new believers who are going to be birthed into the kingdom of God. Remember Jesus' strategy of spiritual parenting; He had the 12, and yet He focused on the 3. Additionally, John was Jesus' closest disciple. Perhaps your core group could be your 3, and your small group could be your 12. Your assistant leader could be your John.

How Spiritual Parenting Multiplies

Paul and Timothy really grasped this truth of spiritual parenting when Paul told Timothy, "You then, my son, be strong in the grace that is in Christ Jesus. And the things you have heard me say in the presence of many witnesses entrust to reliable men who will also be qualified to teach others" (2 Tim. 2:1-2, *NIV*). Paul exhorted Timothy, who was his disciple, to find another reproducing disciple who would then disciple another.

I want to issue you a challenge that has the potential to change the world. Ask God for one reproducing disciple within the next few months. Just one! Sure, if you want to mentor more, go for it as God gives you the grace. But start with one, and encourage your "disciple" to mentor someone else next year. Then the pattern repeats every year as you each find another person to disciple who is also a reproducing disciple. In 10 years, by just mentoring one person each year who is also mentoring one person, you will have been responsible for more than 1,000 people!

After 20 years, at just one disciple per year, how many disciples do you think you would be responsible for? More than 1 million! That's right, more than 1 million in 20 years, at just one person each year. Do the math if you do not believe me. After 30 years, the number jumps to more than 1 billion! No wonder the enemy has been hiding this truth from the Body of Christ and keeping us busy in activity—even religious activity. Now, for the naysayers and doubters who are saying, "But we do not live in a perfect world. What if it breaks down?" My response is simple: "I'll gladly take a half million disciples if it breaks down."

Jesus said it like this: "The good seed represents the people of the Kingdom" (Matt. 13:38). The principles of the Kingdom are found in the parables of the sower (reproducing 30-, 60- and 100-fold) and in the parable of the mustard seed—a seed so small, with so much potential!

God is calling us to a new level of commitment to the dynamic truth of disciplemaking. Recently, I released a two-book biblical foundation series in both English and Spanish titled *Discovering the Basic Truths of Christianity* and *Building Your Life on the Basic Truths of Christianity.* These books are practical tools to help you disciple the next generation by taking just one chapter a week over a year's time and discussing these vital foundational truths with your disciple. When you help others with the basics of Christianity, *you* will also receive renewed faith from His Word to live victoriously above the struggles of daily life.

No matter how talented or experienced you are, if you want to excel at anything, you must practice the fundamentals—the essentials. It's true for playing the piano and for playing baseball or golf, and it's true for the Christian life. Mentoring a young person will bring you back to the basics of Christianity again and again.

So this is my one-person challenge to you: Find your "John" or your "Timothy." Who is your 2 Timothy 2:2 reproducing young disciple going to be?

Learn by Doing

New parents seldom feel equipped to be parents. They learn by doing. It was scary for us when our first child was born. It may be scary for you to take the step of faith to become a spiritual father to someone the Lord brings into your life, but it is a step of obedience that will bring eternal benefits.

Susan, a young mother and a new believer, joined one of our church's small groups expecting to learn biblical values and be encouraged by the time she spent with fellow Christians. But something much greater happened. Liz, an older woman in the group, asked Susan if she wanted to spend time together one-on-one for extra encouragement and accountability. Of course Susan was thrilled. She expected she would listen as Liz taught her all she needed to know about living a victorious Christian life. Liz was such a spiritual giant in Susan's eyes. Not only did she know God's Word, but she was also the most compassionate woman Susan had ever met!

Susan's first surprise was that Liz was so low-key when they met together. She didn't lecture her or act super-spiritual. It was soon apparent that Liz really loved her, as a mother loves her daughter. Bit by bit, Susan opened up her heart to Liz. Liz was easy to talk to because she was transparent in sharing about her own struggles in her marriage, job and family. She taught Susan how to rely on Scripture for answers and prayed with her about everything.

Liz generously and selflessly poured out her life, and Susan blossomed spiritually. A new Christian was brought to maturity because she had a Christlike role model. It happened easily and naturally within a family-type setting of a small group (spiritual family) where she experienced the love and patience of a spiritual parent. Now Susan has taken the step to become a spiritual parent herself, as she has learned to do by Liz's modeling.

Do you expect everyone in your small group to become a spiritual father or mother? If not, you must change your paradigm. Encourage each member to place his or her arms around someone who is younger in the Lord and help them in their journey with Christ. As Elisha experienced a double portion of the Lord's Spirit after being fathered by Elijah, you, too, should expect your spiritual children to go far ahead of you spiritually.

You don't need to be perfect, just faithful and obedient. If you wait until you think you are ready to be the perfect parent, it will never happen.

Small-Group Leaders See the Potential in Others

As a small-group leader you will recognize the undeveloped traits in your group members. Jesus changed Simon's name to Peter, meaning rock. Peter didn't act like a solid, stable rock when he fell asleep in the Garden or denied Jesus three times, but Jesus knew Peter's heart. Peter later became the rock Jesus predicted he would be.

Although small-group leaders cannot predict the future, they can help members set goals and use and develop their gifts so that God will be able to use them to serve Him and others more fully in the future. It should also be noted that Jesus did not nag Peter to grow up after He called him a rock. In Ephesians 6:4, Paul includes this advice to fathers to train their children (see their potential) and not unduly criticize them: "And you, fathers, do not provoke your children to wrath, but bring them up in the training and admonition of the Lord" (*NKJV*). Children will not reach their potential if parents exasperate them with unrealistic expectations or constant criticism.

A spiritual mentor should not be too quick to correct his spiritual son's or daughter's mistakes, or expect too much too soon. Although honesty is important and we cannot overlook a fault if it hinders their walk with the Lord, we should be slow to barge in and correct. Sometimes a mentor will see a weakness but realize the best way for his son to overcome the weakness is for the son to discover it himself. The father simply makes sure he is available to help process the weakness when it surfaces. Instead of pointing out the fault too quickly, we should pray for them and stimulate them with our encouraging words.

Duane was a small-group leader who invited his neighbor Sam, an airline pilot, and his wife, Janice, to their small-group meeting in their home. At first Sam declined the invitation. He wanted nothing to do with Christianity. The Christians he knew were hypocrites and self-righteous. The Christianity he saw was all rules and regulations. He had grown up with a religious background but had been turned off by the church.

But Duane and the other men from the small group persisted in reaching out to Sam. When they saw he was adding a room to his house, they offered to help. Sometime during hammering nails and laying down carpeting, Sam's perception of Christians started to change for the better. These guys were real. They didn't spout a lot of overdone Christian clichés. They admitted their weaknesses and clearly "walked their talk."

Eventually, Sam and Janice both gave their lives to the Lord. The men and women in the small group next door became their spiritual parents. As Sam gave up some bad habits one at a time, the men never condemned him but supported him as a family should.

Today, Sam and Janice lead their own small group of believers. They are now spiritual parents to others.

Small-Group Leaders Are Available

Small-group leaders must be unselfish individuals. They will make themselves accessible and available. Today's society, especially in the Western world, encourages us to be individualistic and selfish with our time. We fill our calendars to the maximum with work-related tasks, but make sure we pencil in generous time slots for recreation and taking care of "Number One."

A mentoring relationship is marked by its liberality. Mentors give of their time generously and sacrificially. With an open heart and hand they purposefully take their spiritual children under their wing.

Start Where You Are

Perhaps you never had a spiritual father or mother. That does not mean you are unable to be one. If you wait until you think you are ready it will probably never happen. You don't need to be perfect, only faithful and obedient. Mother Teresa once said, "God does not demand that I be successful. God demands that I be faithful. When facing God, results are not important. Faithfulness is what is important."[1]

Perhaps you feel that you have already tried and failed. A small-group leader once told me, "After going through a season of discouragement as a leader, I came to understand that God had called me to be a father." This truth set him free as a leader. He realized his primary call was to simply be a spiritual father, and he could trust God for grace to start again when he made mistakes or was discouraged, just like a natural father.

All it takes is willingness, availability, time and a generous dose of the grace of God.

The Bible is filled with examples and models for us to imitate: the impartation from Moses to Joshua; Elijah to Elisha; Samuel to David; Elizabeth to Mary; Paul to Timothy and Titus. We should expect every Christian in our small groups to become a spiritual father or mother as they impart to others what God has given to them. It is possible and achievable!

When a new Christian comes into your group, he or she needs one-on-one discipleship. Obviously, you cannot personally disciple everyone. But you can pray about the possibility of an individual in your small group who could possibly disciple the new believer. If you sense God telling you that Ross could become a friend to and disciple Tom, a new believer, ask Ross to go along with you and Tom to breakfast, or invite both Ross and Tom to your home to see if God would place them together in a relationship. You can be a catalyst in bringing together a potential discipleship relationship. But the Holy Spirit has to do the knitting together of these relationships. You cannot program people. You must pray and encourage them but allow God to bring people together in relationships.

It is especially important that you encourage a new Christian often. He needs daily contact and encouragement for at least a month after he has received Christ, and regular contact for six months to a year. He is a spiritual baby and needs his spiritual "diapers" changed. A new tree is very small, weak and spindly when it's first planted, but it grows larger and stronger. When the roots are grounded, it no longer needs a stake to keep the wind from blowing it over. The same principle applies to new Christians. They need lots of support during their first weeks and months as a Christian.

Becoming a spiritual father or mother is so rewarding! I have had the privilege of being a spiritual father to many generations of leaders and future leaders during the past 40 years.

I started my journey as a spiritual father when I was a chicken farmer in my late teens. And I know that if God can use me, He can certainly use anyone![2]

Now let's look at an almost forgotten mandate in Scripture for all of us and for our small groups: reaching out beyond ourselves and telling others the Good News of Jesus Christ in a genuine, nonreligious way.

Questions for Discussion

1. In your own words, explain how a spiritual father or mother can invest in someone's life.

2. Do you have a spiritual parent in your life? Have you had one in the past? Are you a spiritual parent to another person? Explain.

3. How does spiritual parenting multiply?

Notes
   1. Mother Teresa, cited in *Mother Teresa: In My Own Words*, compiled by Jose Luis Gonzalez-Balado (New York: Random House, 1996), p. 40.
   2. For more about spiritual parenting, read my book *Authentic Spiritual Mentoring* (Ventura, CA: Regal, 2008).

CHAPTER 8

REACH OUT BEYOND YOUR GROUP

Bring Those Who Need to Know Jesus into the Group and Start New Groups

Steve and Debbie were at the end of the line. They knew they had to clean up their act if they ever wanted to see their daughters again. Excessive drug use had caused them to lose their business, their home, their cars, and their three daughters to Child Protection Services. They desperately wanted to see their children again, so they were in the process of relocating to get a new start on life and to be close to their daughters who were in the guardianship of Debbie's father.

Bob, a small-group leader, met the couple as he walked into the YMCA in his hometown. He recalls, "I sensed the Lord wanted me to help them in some way. So I introduced myself, gave them my phone number and offered whatever help I could. Their story soon poured out. Debbie was pregnant, they had only $20 left and they were living in an old van they had purchased for $25. Steve and Debbie were looking for a place to clean up, so our small group offered to help them in their move and getting resettled.

"Later that day, Steve called, and we invited them to our home group. They came that very night and surrendered their lives to Jesus! Steve received a position with a paving contractor, as a blade operator. Along with the position, the company let them rent a four-bedroom house on the property for only $150 per month. Steve and Debbie have not only been drug free, they have seen the salvation of their God as He provided for them in many astounding ways, including being reunited with their children. What great joy in the family and small group!"

Although different small groups may have different purposes for existing, we have found that a primary focus of small groups should be, in most cases, both discipleship and outreach. Many times small groups focus only on fellowship, which usually leads to a stagnant group. They forget about the importance of reaching others for Christ. Jesus Himself said, "I have come to seek and save that which was lost" (see Luke 19:10). There are hurting people all around us. And although great fellowship is certainly important, it will be a healthy by-product of the group that has learned to reach out to others.

Within a group there will be much prayer and interaction to meet needs and form relationships, but the top priority must always be to bring in those who do not yet know Jesus. This will also cause the group to mature and multiply or reproduce another group. There is nothing like bringing a new baby into a home. The siblings grow up quickly by focusing on the needs of the new child, and they get their eyes off of their own selfish needs. Reaching out to others will give more believers the opportunity to use the gifts the Lord has given them to reach out and make disciples.

The greatest catalyst I know of to grow in Christ is to get our eyes off of ourselves and instead look to Jesus and to the needs of those around us. A group of people who are always looking inward and are content to have the status quo will probably never grow and multiply. Looking inward prevents growth, like an ingrown toenail, and usually causes pain, competition and stagnation.

When groups are content to stay the same, they unwittingly build a wall around themselves, causing others to feel they are not welcome. The group that has a heart to reach out to others is willing to change, and enjoys wonderful fellowship in the process.

When I was newly married and a young missionary, I heard a man of God quote C. T. Studd, the famous missionary: "I do not wish to live 'neath sound of church or chapel bell; I want to run a rescue shop within a yard of hell." These words were life-changing for me.

The main purpose for a small group is to run a rescue shop within a yard of hell. Otherwise, the group becomes a social club without any power. The Lord gives us power to be His witnesses, not to sit around and enjoy nice, comfortable "bless me" meetings.

There will be many different creative approaches to reaching out and making disciples as we work together in a small-group setting; however, the primary vision must be clear and fixed. We are called to fulfill the Great Commission. The main focus of our vision should be to seek the Lord for creative ways to reach pre-Christians and make disciples.

One small group I was a part of printed up an attractive flyer with a photo of our smiling group. One summer we canvassed the neighborhood where we met. We handed out the flyer to those who were newcomers to the community, along with a houseplant to welcome the new families and invite them to the group.

Some youth small groups have used clowning as a regular outreach ministry for their small group. Dressed as clowns, they go to hospitals, parks or visit the elderly and generally spread cheer and the gospel wherever they go as they hand out balloons and do short skits.

Picnic evangelism is an informal way to reach family and friends with the message of the gospel. Small-group members take the initiative to invite friends and relatives to a picnic that includes free food, games and entertainment. Through the outreach of these family-oriented picnics, relationships are built and people come to Christ.

One small group discussed how they could care for people who were traveling through a long, hard journey and find a way to refresh them. The Lord showed them three families they knew who were facing difficulties. The group planned an elegant candle-lit dinner for a middle-aged couple, to give them a much-needed break. They collected money for a young widow so she could go out for dinner and shopping while the small group baby-sat her four children. For another widow, they felt led to wrap small gifts and deliver them in a pretty basket. She invited the group to pray with her and shared that her daughter was in prison and needed prayer support. This was an opportunity the group felt God laid in their laps. They started to write to the daughter and pray for her regularly.

David's small group was challenged to find ways to reach those who do not know Jesus, and God gave David a natural opportunity. He says, "Recently, I noticed a banner flapping in the breeze off the back porch of a house near where I live. It was for the college football team I follow, the Miami Hurricanes. The thought came to me, *Walk up there and introduce yourself.* Several days later, I walked the 15 minutes to the home and rang the doorbell. A man, about my age, came to the door. Then for the next 45 minutes, we talked about growing up in Florida, college football and life in Kentucky. We started a relationship. There is no real spiritual life evident in this man's life. A new relationship is forming and God is giving me a new opportunity to be a witness of Jesus."

When small groups and individuals have evangelism as an integral part of their focus, God often brings nonbelievers right into their small-group settings. Wendy befriended Susi, an atheist German exchange student at her school. She invited Susi along to her small group, and over the next several months, Susi soaked in God's Word and asked many challenging questions of her newfound friends. It was an exciting day for the entire group when Susi announced she had made Jesus the Lord of her life and wanted to be baptized.

When individuals in small groups challenge each other to reach beyond themselves to make disciples, they will discover that God will give them many creative opportunities. Even if no one immediately comes to Christ through these opportunities, there is a spiritual dynamic released in the group that keeps their focus on the harvest fields instead of on themselves. As we continue to sow, we will eventually reap.

The *Oikos* Principle

When I served as a pastor, a group from our church took a trip to Seoul, Korea, to visit the largest church in the world, Yoido Full Gospel Church. They had literally thousands of small groups in their church. One of the principles that we learned during our time there was the "*oikos* principle."

What is an *oikos*? Acts 10:2 speaks of Cornelius and all of his family (*oikos*). *Oikos* is the Greek word for household or house of people. Your *oikos* is that group of people with whom you relate on a regular basis. All believers should apply the *oikos* principle to their lives as a way of infiltrating their spheres of influence with the gospel of Jesus Christ.

One time when Paul and Silas were in prison, in the midst of an earthquake the jailer became receptive to the gospel. He invited his household to listen to Paul's message and they were all saved. This group of people was his *oikos*. The *oikos* principle is a strategy of using our existing relationships to evangelize and to make disciples. This includes:

- Family and relatives. Your Uncle Jack and Aunt Sadie and cousin Ted are all part of your *oikos*, even if they live far away. If you maintain regular contact with them, they are part of your *oikos*.

- Those who have common interests with you. Those who play tennis with you are part of your *oikos*. Anyone you share a common interest with, such as an interest in computers, sewing, playing basketball, playing the guitar—these people are a part of your *oikos*.

- Those who live in the same geographical location as you. Your neighbors are a part of your *oikos*.

- Those who have a common vocation. Those with whom you work—your fellow employees—are a part of your *oikos*. If you are a construction worker, your *oikos* includes other construction workers. If you are a doctor, other professional people that you relate with would be included in your *oikos*.

- Others with whom you have regular contact. These people may include your dentist, family doctor, mechanic, hairdresser, sales people, school officials, and the like.

Those people in your *oikos* group will be much more receptive to the gospel in God's timing because they trust you—you have built a relationship with them.

Amy, a young woman in Indiana, started talking to Jim, a fellow engineer at work, about the Lord. He would share struggles he was having with his family, opening the door for her to share Jesus with him. Here's her story describing how her *oikos* relationship grew to include her small group as they worked together to reach this family.

One day, I could tell something was really troubling Jim. He told me that his father, Jim Sr., was dying and how difficult it was on the entire family. In fact, his father had been asking about God lately. He was afraid to die.

Immediately, I began to pray, "Oh Father, give me wisdom what to do!" Our small group's desire was to reach out to our *oikos*—the people we relate to on a daily basis—and I realized this was a wide-open door for our group to pray. From my computer, I emailed everyone in my group, asking them to start praying that the Lord would give me wisdom how to reach this man and his family.

My small group was extremely supportive. Within one hour, I received two emails from members who were praying for me. One of my small-group members, Julie, also knew Jim personally because she used to work with us. So I called her to see if she would go with me to pray for Jim's father. She was excited at the opportunity to share Jesus with someone who desperately needed hope.

At work the next day, I asked Jim if we could pray with his father. He was very open to the idea. He called his parents, and they too were thrilled to hear we were coming. Of course, I jumped back on my computer and emailed my small group to start praying again!

That night, Julie and I drove to Jim Sr.'s house. When we arrived, Jim Sr., his wife, Sandy, and their granddaughter, Nicole, were there. They were so hospitable as we talked for a while, getting to know them.

When we asked them what they would like us to pray for, Jim Sr. said he was afraid to die— he was afraid of the unknown. Julie began to talk about the assurance we can have through Jesus Christ. Then I shared the concepts of salvation and eternal life with him. After discussing some more, we had the privilege of leading Jim Sr. to receive Jesus as his personal Savior. What a blessing this was for us!

At work the next day, Jim thanked me for praying with his parents. I told him it was our pleasure, meanwhile thinking to myself, *You're next!* I mentioned that our group offered to bring over dinner for his family or help them with other daily chores. He was amazed that people who didn't even know him would offer to help his family.

My group made dinner, and I took it to their house. The next day at work, Jim Jr. couldn't stop thanking me for the dinner. I told him it was my small group that made the dinner and we all have been praying for them. Later that day, he asked me for directions so he could bring his family to our group!

Everyone in my small group is praying for this family. Though I am the one with the closest working relationship with this family, we all play a role—especially one of prayer. This is what small-group life is all about! Working together to reach the lost!

Sometimes Christians discover they have only other believers in their *oikos*. When this is the case, steps need to be taken to develop new circles of relationships. Some believers join soccer teams, neighborhood organizations and other community groups to increase their *oikos*.

More than 30 years ago, when LaVerne and I and a group of young people began to play baseball, basketball and other sports with youth in our local community, we built relationships with them and they became a part of our *oikos*. Because we established friendships with them on their turf, we could readily share the good news of Jesus. Our *oikos* is part of God's strategy to reach the world.

Small-group members have many everyday *oikos* opportunities. Our small group has many first-generation Christians. And most of them came to our group and to Christ due to being friends of a young man in our group who gave his life to Christ.

Bob's story is another example that illustrates how an entire family *oikos* was impacted with the gospel. After Bob and his wife found new life and stability in Christ, Bob was burdened for his parents, brothers and sisters who were far from God. Bob, along with his small group, prayed that God would allow him to contact his father, with whom the family had lost contact. Although the situation seemed hopeless, through a series of miracles Bob reached his dad. His dad was living with Bob's half-sister, and they both received Jesus into their lives. Bob and his sister traveled to another state to share the message of the hope Jesus offers with her brother, and he and his wife made a decision to follow Christ. Continuing on to yet another state, Bob contacted his mother, and she responded immediately, "I want to accept Jesus." It helped that Bob's oldest brother had accepted the Lord a few days earlier. Looking back on it, Bob is sure that the Spirit of God moved so freely in response to the many prayers of the believers praying for Bob's "miracle missionary outreach" to his family *oikos*.

The *oikos* strategy is the most natural way of fulfilling the Great Commission. Nearly every Christian has at least 20 people in his or her *oikos*. These 20 people plus their *oikos* gives the potential of 400 contacts (20 x 20). People want the truth! They are waiting for real Christians they can trust to give them the truth of the gospel.

You may want to write down your *oikos*. Pray and ask God to show you two or three of the people you're most concerned about and begin to pray for these people and reach out to them. If they are unsaved, you will be involved in evangelism. If they are struggling in their Christian lives, God may call you to be involved in discipleship. Either way, you are called to pray for them.

One small-group leader shared his faith in Christ with a salesman who came into his place of business. Later the salesman received the Lord and got involved with believers in a small group in his neighborhood. The small group began to pray for the salesman's unsaved mother. She received the Lord a few weeks before she passed away.

Small groups that understand the *oikos* principle realize it is a very natural way to fulfill the Great Commission. And new persons coming to Christ prepare the way for new small groups to be birthed.

Growing and Starting New Groups

The process of multiplication in human cells is called mitosis. It is multiplication by dividing. One cell becomes two, and each continues to grow until they, too, divide and separate to become four cells.

In the same way, each small group needs to go through a period of gestation (growth and learning) before it can give birth to a new group. When a new small group starts, the first months are a good time for building relationships.

During the next few months there should be more of an emphasis on bringing others into the small group. Share with friends, neighbors, those at work and with loved ones about how Jesus has changed your life. Tell them what is going on—what God is doing in your group. Expect people to come to a place of faith in Jesus Christ.

As a small-group leader, you should continue to give a clear vision that the small group will eventually multiply. Then, as the group gets larger, the people will begin to talk about birthing a new group. I was a member of one small group that became large and cumbersome. We decided to meet in smaller groups for prayer during our meetings. A month or two later we decided to take these four prayer groups and meet in separate homes. We were still a part of the same large group, but we met at times as smaller prayer meetings in different homes instead of always attending the regular small-group meeting as often as we had before. After doing this for a while, some of the small prayer groups became so excited about their small group that they decided to begin a new home group. It is said that some people never learn to swim until they jump into the water! The same is true with small-group multiplication.

It goes without saying that there should be a lot of prayer and open communication about specific upcoming changes. Give the people some time to get used to the new idea until it is birthed in their own hearts and they welcome it. Then it will not be a traumatic thing, but something that everyone looks forward to with enthusiasm and faith. Encourage each person to seek the Lord's wisdom on any proposed change and get back to you with a response. It is best if the move can be confirmed by as many people in the group as possible. During this time the leaders should be accountable to the local church leaders who will pray with them and assist them.

Remember, growth is healthy. A healthy church is a growing church—numerically, by adding people to His kingdom, and in maturity, by growing closer to our Lord Jesus.

"How often should a small group multiply?" is one of the questions that I am most often asked by pastors and small-group leaders. The answer depends on what the Holy Spirit is saying to you and in what culture you are living.

In our culture, we believe that believers in every small group should ask the Lord for the grace to spawn a new group each year. Other cultures and nations could be much more often. Encouraging each group to multiply each year is a goal to encourage; however, we do not make it a requirement. Many groups will have the grace to multiply more often than once a year.

Goals are important, but they must be birthed by the Holy Spirit and attainable. The key to the timing of multiplying groups is when new leaders have been called by God and trained to take on this new responsibility.

When it is time for a group to multiply, the small-group members will be ready for it because they were preparing for this process all along. Often a small group has been praying for a particular town or area, and a few members who live there subsequently feel called to begin a new group in that city. Because assistant leaders have been raised up previously in the small group, this can provide ongoing leadership potential to accommodate multiplication.

And remember, the purpose for multiplication in the small group is to see God's people released to train others and fulfill God's Word (see 2 Tim. 2:2), not just to meet a goal.

I wish I could promise you that leading a small group is always easy. I would not be telling you the truth if I said that. Leading a small group is, however, very rewarding. It is a bit like raising children. I never tell new parents that raising children is always going to be easy, but I often tell them it is certainly rewarding. Now, in the next chapter, let's look at some of the challenges you may face as small-group leaders.

Questions for Discussion

1. Why should outreach be a focus of a small group?

2. If a small group loses sight of outreach, what is the natural tendency of that group?

3. Make a list of persons you currently have in your *oikos*. How can you focus on them and reach out to them?

CHAPTER 9

DEALING WITH DIFFICULT PEOPLE

How to Help People Who Do Not Want to Change

Patricia showed up at the small group without warning one evening with three squirming, unkempt and disruptive children. She was not shy about sharing her needs with the group, and it wasn't long before this disgruntled woman had our attention. Life seemed impossible for her—overdue bills, rowdy children and an overwhelming marriage to a long-distance truck driver.

In time, we realized that Patricia's problem was not her seemingly unbearable life, but an addiction. She was addicted to people and the attention they could give. It was not uncommon for Patricia to spend a whole day stationed in the kitchen of an unsuspecting small-group member. She gravitated toward people who showed any interest in her life-controlling problems. As time went on, many couples and individuals who tried to minister to Patricia suffered burnout. No one could ever seem to do enough for her or her family.

Patricia did not show a desire to come closer to Jesus or to be discipled. What she did desire was to have the uncomfortable things in her life "fixed" by the care-takers and responsible ones within the small group. Patricia wanted to be rescued and cared for. The truth is that we could give and give to Patricia and her family (which we initially attempted to do), but nothing or no one could fill the emotional void in her life. Recognizing this from the beginning could have spared many well-meaning people from becoming burned out.

As a small-group leader, you may have experienced someone like Patricia who is attracted to your group or to you as a leader because his or her basic needs of love and acceptance, security and intimacy are unmet. These are legitimate needs, and while it is true that the small group can provide love, support and acceptance, it is not appropriate that the small group or small-group leader become the sole source to meet these needs. The natural outgrowth of relationships developing within the small group will provide for some emotional needs but can never replace the natural family, parents or a spouse.

While a small group provides support, it is not a support group like Alcoholics Anonymous. We overstep our boundaries when we find ourselves wanting to provide for the security or intimacy needs of another.

Two Core Needs: Security and Significance

As a small-group leader, are we called to counsel others? The answer is both yes and no. No, in that we are not called to be professional people helpers. Answering yes, however, defines our roles and our purposes in helping hurting individuals within our small group. The key lies in Colossians 1:28: "We proclaim him, admonishing and teaching everyone with all wisdom, so that we may *present everyone perfect in Christ*" (*NIV*, emphasis added). It was Paul, the apostle, who calls us to labor in this way, and it is where we must spend our energy.

This verse could be succinctly paraphrased *to build the life of Christ*. The apostle Paul calls us to labor in this way, and we must spend our energy in following his wisdom. Our goal must be to build the life of Christ into people with problems in our group rather than take on the role of therapist.

But where do we begin? Christian psychologist Larry Crabb says there are two core needs that all of us are attempting to have met in our lives: security and significance. Think back to that last small-group meeting when a member was pouring his or her heart out with a need. Often, at the core of the person's very being is a need for security: knowing that he belongs, is accepted, approved of without condition, and loved. Or she has the need of significance: knowing that she is important and what she does in life is important to her small-group family and others.

Here's the really great news. Jesus is the "Wonderful Counselor" (Isa. 9:6, *NIV*), and when we have Him and His Word, we are armed with the truth. Colossians 1:12-22 and Ephesians 1:4-14 are Scripture passages that describe our security and significance in Christ. Perhaps a parent rejected him, a husband abandoned her, drugs and alcohol stole years of his life, or abuse wounded her soul. Nevertheless, as small-group members begin to speak the love of Christ, the approval of Christ, the redemption, the adoption, the grace, the forgiveness, the reconciliation and the justification of the life of Christ, a Patricia can begin to be put back together again.

Our need for security and significance is tied into our relationships. Unhealthy relationships are those in which one person constantly strives to receive from another or from a group. The hurting person's quest is for a particular need to be provided for, healed, supported. A healthy relationship occurs when two people are offering the good to the other. The question they are asking is, "What can I do to support the other person, love him, serve him and provide for his needs?" This is the act of building the life of Christ.

If a relationship is built on what someone thinks she can receive to build herself up, the relationship will eventually die. Unhealthy small-group members want their needs to be met by those in the group they perceive as healthy, but most of those who seem healthy need healing themselves.

The Rule of the Spirit

First Thessalonians 5:23 reveals, "May God himself, the God of peace, sanctify you through and through. May your whole *spirit, soul and body* be kept blameless at the coming of our Lord Jesus Christ" (*NIV*, emphasis added). We feed our bodies with three or more meals a day. We feed the soul with years of schooling, but we often neglect the spirit. I believe the change that everyone desires comes from the Spirit of God. Our bodies and our minds cannot be in charge of our spirit. Our spirit must lead the way to change.

Hurting individuals often want someone else to relieve their pain or be their cure. If you let yourself become the medicine, you can create an unhealthy emotional dependency. Jesus must become the source of security and significance—there is no other Savior. Paul reminds us in Galatians 1:10 that our identity does not come from man, but from God. "Am I now trying to win the approval of men, or of God?" (*NIV*; see also 1 Thess. 2:4-6).

Romans 8:5-7 is a very clear and helpful Scripture that exposes the battle between the soul and the spirit: "Those who live according to the sinful nature have their minds set on what that nature desires; but those who live in accordance with the Spirit have their minds set on what the Spirit desires. The mind of sinful man is death, but the mind controlled by the Spirit is life and peace; the sinful mind is hostile to God. It does not submit to God's law, nor can it do so" (*NIV*).

Change begins when the Spirit of God is given control of our spirit, soul and body. Ryan had no boundaries in his life. He spent hours on the phone with or at the houses of unsuspecting small-group members. His neediness drove him to those he thought could fill his emotional cup. It was an emotional cup that was insatiable. The Ryans and Patricias in small groups must be taught and shown models that portray that our spirits (controlled by God's Spirit) must teach our minds—not our minds teach our spirits. The intellect and the emotional self is to submit to the rule of the Spirit.

Loving Limits

A second key to building the life of Christ is providing boundaries or limits. Often these limits have not been instilled in those whose lives revolve around their self-esteem needs. Boundaries are all around us: doors, walls, fences, sidewalks and yellow lines on the highway.

Personal boundaries are harder to see but just as necessary to a person's overall well-being.

Help a hurting person identify appropriate and sometimes new boundaries. Jesus had boundaries for His disciples (see Matt. 6). In John 4, Jesus did not rescue the woman at the well. Instead He revealed to her that she was attempting to get her needs met in men. She was even living with a man who was not her husband. She had crossed a boundary that had been set in Scripture, and she needed to live within the boundaries set by God before she would be ready to accept Christ's offer of salvation.

Boundaries are limits, and when God imposes these limits, they are healthy limits. Help people identify within Scripture those guidelines that their heavenly Father is lovingly providing for them.

Within the small group, people may need help setting practical boundaries such as: who they can visit, how long they can stay, how often they can phone, how many times they should expect others to baby-sit for them, and how much the group can give when there is a financial need. Boundaries will help needy people and provide limits for people who want to help.

Challenging False Beliefs

Our thoughts stem from our beliefs. Some of our thoughts will be true and some will be lies.

One evening, during a small-group meeting of our church, a couple shared a tragic experience they had in a former church and how it deeply hurt them. While the experience was true and their feelings real, they spoke something from their belief about this church and its leaders that was very hurtful. Their small-group leader made a mental note of their poisonous comment and confronted them before they left for the evening. The husband received the input and acknowledged that the comment stemmed from their hurt. The wife refused to hear the leader or retract her statement. A belief had formed from her life experience, and she was unable to let go of the feelings and reactions to her thoughts.

You may eventually hear comments like: "The last church I was in gave up on me, and you will too" or "I've been in three rehabs and two psych wards, and they told me I was a hopeless case" or "My parents kicked me out of the house when I was 15." There may be some partial truth found in these statements, but much of what they presently tell themselves stems from major misbeliefs.

Wellness: Everyone's Choice

How can a hurting person be healed? By the truth—because the truth sets us free. Consider Jesus' ministry. When Jesus confronted the invalid at the pool of Bethesda in John 5, he asked the man an interesting question. John 5:6 states, "When Jesus saw him lying there and learned that he had been in this condition for a long time [38 years], he asked him, 'Do you want to get well?'" (*NIV*).

Visualize this: the lame man is at the pool where all of the disabled—the blind, the lame, the paralyzed—are hanging out. They are most likely discussing the usual stuff. One of them is wondering if they would have barley soup for supper again. Another is complaining about how few times the angel shows up to "stir" the water.

Perhaps a young boy is lamenting the fact that he will never play sports like other kids. The paralytic of 38 years is just commenting about how tough it is to find someone to help him to the water, and if he does find someone, it is always too late—another needy one reaches the pool before him.

Life is rough around that pool; then again, no one has to work. Perhaps they are guaranteed several hot meals a day. They have their friends. There is a certain amount of security being a part of this disabled bunch. They have a lot in common.

Then the Savior comes along and asks that controversial question. Maybe to the invalid He is really asking, "Do you want to change?" Consider the ramifications: he would have to leave his home of 38 years (perhaps he is somewhat of a peer leader); he would need to become productive and provide for himself; he would no longer have excuses to not make changes in his life.

Jesus confronted this person's beliefs with the opportunity to begin a new life through a healing of his physical body and a transformation of his beliefs.

There are or will be small-group members who do not want to be well. They only know how to live life by walking within the world they know. While change seems inviting, it is so unfamiliar to them that it is a place of insecurity they fear. They decide to remain in their present state, as broken as it may be, experiencing what some call the "tyranny of the familiar."

What About Resolving Conflict?

Whenever you work with people, eventually there will be conflict. Here are a few biblical steps that have helped me deal with conflict in an effective way. I personally do not like conflict, and I find that most people are just like me in this regard. But conflicts are a part of what we have to deal with as small-group leaders. Let's look at some systematic principles to resolve conflict. Remember, conflict is not necessarily bad. People in your small group may be leaders who are often strong personalities who have been successful in business or ministry and other areas of life because of boldly following what they believe is right.

We need to learn to defer to each other. We must patiently learn to listen, forgive, receive, rebuke, correct and submit to each other. We need to be more concerned about being understanding than being understood. But even with these patterns in place, conflicts will occur. Sometimes the conflicts are about a specific subject, and other times they may be about personalities and needs. James 4:1 reveals that our conflicts come from our desires. We want something different from what God desires. No matter what their origin, when conflicts occur, a leader's response should be to discern the reasons behind the conflict and the needs of those involved. In my book *21 Tests of Effective Leadership,* I give the following principles that apply to resolving conflict.[1]

1. Gain Agreement that a Problem Exists
First, we must listen to each others' views on the subject at hand so it is clear as to what the conflict really is about. Define what issues are involved in the conflict and for whom it is a conflict. Pray for discernment to be able to detect any possible hidden issues in the disagreement.

In approaching the problem situation, we should begin by asking questions to draw the other(s) out.

Statements tend to push people apart. Instead, ask questions. Try to understand the other's point of view. Try to find out what is behind each opinion. This helps another person see that you are willing to accept responsibility if you have contributed to the conflict.

Dialogue should use these kinds of phrases: "When you . . . I feel . . . because . . ." For example, "When you speak in that tone of voice, I feel like you are devaluing me because you are treating me like a child." This lets the other party know how you feel when the conflict is occurring.

Let the other person know how you react to the conflict. Listen for the feelings and emotions of the other and reflect on them with empathy and understanding. This creates an atmosphere of being cared for and listened to. It reduces defensiveness and focuses on the process involved rather than on the issues.

2. Identify the Consequences Up Front

Ask yourself, *What is the worst possible consequence if this conflict is never addressed and resolved?* One thing you should be able to agree on immediately is that if the conflict goes unresolved, it may lead to division on the team. This helps warn the group that the conflict should not be allowed to fester or remain unresolved.

Paul addressed dissension in the early church by appealing for them to make an adjustment so that unity could prevail. He encouraged them to take immediate measures to repair their disagreements before strife tore them apart. "I appeal to you, dear brothers and sisters, by the authority of our Lord Jesus Christ, to live in harmony with each other. Let there be no divisions in the church. Rather, be of one mind, united in thought and purpose" (1 Cor. 1:10). When conflict is resolved, the team will reap the benefit of "harmony with each other."

3. Pray Together in Faith

Pray and ask the Lord to help you discern the reasons behind the conflict and what to do about it. "If you need wisdom, ask our generous God, and he will give it to you" (Jas. 1:5). Praying is a powerful way of seeking agreement. Sometimes the solution is revealed during the prayer time.

4. Mutually Agree on an Action

Too often we spend most of our time on the conflict and forget to pursue possible solutions. Make a list of any proposed action (solution). Then pray over the list and pick an action (possible solution) that everyone agrees with. Believe in faith for a win-win solution as you approach possible solutions together. "Can two people walk together without agreeing on the direction?" (Amos 3:3). Will the proposed action allow a healing process to begin with no one being blamed? Does it provide for an end of the conflict, with no recurrence? Will it result in better understanding by all parties with all feelings being respected? There is power in unity, and when we can agree on an action, the blessings of "life" the Lord promises in Psalm 133 will flow into the situation.

5. Follow Up and Measure Progress

Allow for a period of evaluation to determine if the resolution is successful in averting similar conflict(s). Set a specific date to meet and review the resolution and determine to alter the resolution if it is not working.

Once a conflict has been resolved and all the parties feel like they have been listened to, cared for and understood, then it is time to "let go" of the conflict. The individuals involved should put the conflict behind them and forget it. Don't bring it up in the future. God does not remember our sins to hold them against us, and we should do the same.

6. Ask for Help if the Conflict Cannot Be Resolved

If the conflict cannot be resolved, look for help from an objective, trusted outsider. God is a God of restoration, and the goal of any conflict is always restoration. If you find yourself at an impasse, an objective outsider, preferably a trusted spiritual advisor or pastor or coach, can be brought in to help resolve the issue. Every person who has authority needs to be under authority. A conflict between leaders that cannot be resolved goes to the leaders who have appointed them and given them oversight. They have the God-given authority to bring resolution. "Obey your spiritual leaders, and do what they say. Their work is to watch over your souls, and they are accountable to God. Give them reason to do this with joy and not with sorrow. That would certainly not be for your benefit" (Heb. 13:17).

You Can Do It!

You and your small-group members can be involved in helping people by infusing the Spirit of God in them, creating and setting appropriate boundaries with them, and challenging any false beliefs with the truth of God's Word.

We must pray for the hurting, believe for them and know that there is always hope. We serve a life-changing Redeemer. Do you recall walking through very troubling times early in your Christian life? What helped you? How did others reach out to you? Be assured that some of these very same helping principles will also help the Ryans and Patricias in your small group.

As a small-group leader, you are a "people helper" who can provide effective counsel. Your competency comes from God and your ability to love others. Hebrews 10:24-25 says, "Let us think of ways to motivate one another to acts of love and good works. And let us not neglect our meeting together, as some people do, but encourage one another, especially now that the day of his return is drawing near."[2]

Questions for Discussion

1. How do you begin to build the life of Christ in another?

2. Why are the core needs of security and significance so important in people's lives?

3. Why is it so important to let go of a conflict and resolve it within the small group?

Notes
1. Larry Kreider, *21 Tests of Effective Leadership* (Shippensburg, PA: Destiny Image Publishers, 2010).
2. Thanks to my colleague Steve Prokopchak for this excerpt (first half of chapter) from his *People Helping People* series on emotional dependency and his book *Counseling Basics: Helping You Help Others* (Lititz, PA: House to House Publications, 2004).

CHAPTER 10

PRACTICAL TIPS FOR SMALL-GROUP LEADERS

Become a More Effective Leader

Tears were streaming down Tami's happy face as she reached for Bob's hand. "Who gives this woman to this man in marriage before God and this family of witnesses?"

Just weeks earlier, Tami and Bob had given their lives to Jesus. They had been living together, unmarried, and now wanted to be married before God and their friends and family. Their small group wanted them to have a wedding to remember. The group helped them plan their wedding celebration, from sewing Tami's wedding gown, right down to putting the last swirl on the wedding cake's frosting.

Bob and Tami were beginning a new adventure to-gether—commitment to married life along with learn-ing to encourage, pray and bear each other's burdens within a small-group setting. Their small group's ac-tion of serving them was teaching Bob and Tami that their fellowship with God also brought them into fel-lowship with a community of believers who would ac-tively support them and guide them more fully in the ways of Christ.

That's what small groups are all about—helping others encounter a loving community within the group. As a leader, you help make that happen!

Helping new Christians, like Bob and Tami, can be messy, but if new believers are not allowed to make mistakes and learn, they will not grow spiritually. Proverbs 14:4 says, "Where no oxen are, the trough is clean; but much increase comes by the strength of an ox" (*NKJV*). Even Lazarus came out of the grave with some grave clothes still hanging on.

As a leader, you can set the example by loving and accepting all people in the group, regardless of their spiritual maturity. Perhaps the best philosophy in relating to new Christians is to try to always expect the best, but accept the worst. The general atmosphere of love and acceptance in a small group is a safe place for individuals to step out and try new things. Expect new Christians to do great things, but be there for them if they crash and burn. This support is very important.

Hospitality

Practicing New Testament hospitality is critical to experiencing New Testament church life. Small-group ministry without hospitality becomes mundane and programmatic. As a leader, set the example by practicing hospitality!

Hospitality is a wonderful gift given to us to minister to others. Hospitality is something that must be practiced. Our homes are remarkable tools to minister to others. We do not need to serve elaborate meals. We can be free to keep it simple. We can order pizza! The key is our availability.

Jesus said to Simon, "You gave Me no water for My feet, but she has washed My feet with her tears" (Luke 7:44, *NKJV*). Pray that people will feel their feet have been washed; they have been refreshed by being in your home. The difference between hospitality and entertaining is that entertaining says, "I want to impress." It puts things before people. Entertainment looks for payment and compliments. Hospitality says, "I want to minister. This is not my own show." Hospitality will put people before things and will not look for reward. Small groups that do not practice hospitality only have meetings!

Is it ever right to say no? Yes! Jesus did. He knew His priorities (see Mark 1:32-38). Remember to not practice hospitality by yourself. Find people to help you—especially those who have a gift of hospitality. Encourage everyone in your group to practice hospitality.

Helping in Times of Crisis

All of us experience times of crisis. A crisis is an opportune time for the small group to get actively involved in ministering to others. If someone in your group is going through a crisis, you should activate the members of your group to serve the person as you see appropriate.

When a storm brought a huge tree crashing down on their house roof, one family at our church immediately experienced God's love in action through their small group. "Love started flowing our way the very next day in the form of a tub of brownies and help to remove the tree from the roof," they reported. "Brownies don't solve a mess, but they sure lift your spirits!" One evening everyone from the small group helped to repair water damage to the inside of the house. They hung a drop ceiling, painted, fixed a door and did electrical work and many other smaller jobs. This family's misfortune was turned to a blessing as the small group had the opportunity to "do it unto Jesus" as they helped bear this family's burdens.

During times of crisis or change in someone's life, it's important to respond with an attitude of love, gentleness and compassion. A storm-torn house, a change of jobs, the death of a loved one, a house move, the birth of a baby are all types of change that add extra pressure to our lives.

Remember, faith works by love. As you identify with the person's situation, God will show you how to best respond. The Lord has called us to all work together to build the Body of Christ.

Here are a few examples of what you can do when someone in your group is going through the following crisis or change:

- *Hospitalization*: provide prayer, visitation, calls to family, flowers, childcare, housesitting. Contact your pastor to let him know of the hospitalization, especially in the case of an extended or serious illness.

- *Illness:* If a person is absent from the meeting due to illness, the entire group should be encouraged to pray for the sick, visit, take meals to the family, provide transportation, and send cards and flowers.

- *Financial need:* If someone has a financial or material need, you may want to initiate a special offering to help meet the need. If it is greater than the group can meet, the need should be discussed with your pastor or spiritual over-seer. In many of our churches the congregations have a "deacon's fund." This fund receives a percentage of the monies that are given to the church through the weekly tithes as well as special designated offerings. All monies that are in the deacon's fund are set apart to help those who have special financial needs, and these funds are administered through the small groups, which provide a sense of accountability.

- *A house move:* When someone moves to another house or location, the small-group leader can set the standard as a servant and give leadership to the others within the group who are assisting in moving a family or a single person from one location to another. Encourage the group to assist with packing, moving, childcare and meals. It can be a great time of fellowship for your group! The responsibility for organizing the move day, including helping to line up trucks, should be delegated to others within the group as much as is possible; however, as a small-group leader, you should take the responsibility to make sure that it happens.

- *Death in the family:* Be sensitive to the needs of the family. Pray for them and serve in whatever way you can. In our church, local pastors will serve with the small-group leader during these times of crisis. Due to the leader's close relationship with the family that has experienced a death, he may receive the information before the local pastor. If this happens, leaders are encouraged to contact the pastor immediately. Ask the pastor how the group can effectively help the family during this time.

- *New baby:* Set up a schedule to provide meals for the family. Perhaps you can baby-sit some of the other children in the family during this time and set up a schedule for others within the group to serve in this way.

- *Discover your small group's purpose:* Each small-group family has its own personality and focus. Remember, without a progressive vision, God's people perish (see Prov. 29:18). Without a clear vision of what the Father is doing in your group, there is a tendency to become lethargic. Do not allow it to happen! Expect to experience the life of Christ among you!

One small group, with a Spanish-speaking leader, Arturo, knew from the start that God had placed them near the mushroom farms in Reading, Pennsylvania, for a reason: to cultivate relationships with the Mexican migrant workers living and working there. Dorothy, a member of the group, describes her first encounter reaching out cross-culturally.

On our initial visit as a small group, I was a bit anxious. I spoke only English. How could I show my love to these people without the most basic of communication—language? Of course, it helped that we were doing this as a group. And we knew God had called us for this purpose.

On our first visit to the farms, I met Bernardo, who was working in his garden. Even with a language barrier, there was instant rapport as I shared my own love of gardening by pointing out the different seedlings and identifying them with Bernardo. Then we shared with a larger group of workers, telling them that God cared about their tears and loneliness in a strange place. The love God poured out that day was tangible!

My husband and I had so much fun, we couldn't wait to go back. Since that first contact, our small group has made many friends at the farms. Pizza parties, Bible studies and English classes are part of our regular activities with the workers. Seven men have prayed the sinner's prayer and are being discipled by members in our group.

Your small group should find what its unique purpose is within the plan of God, and then follow that mandate. The most common type of small groups at our church consists of a mixed group with a balance of families, young and older people and singles. These groups may have a mission of intercession, praying actively for people in their communities and the church. Others periodically serve at local rescue missions or serve the homeless. Still others may spend time ministering to lonely senior citizens at the nursing home.

Reaching Out to the Unchurched

There are a few small groups that have reached out solely to the unchurched children in their communities. They are convinced that today's kids have vast spiritual needs and must be led into an early and deeply meaningful relationship with Jesus Christ before their tender hearts are hardened by the world. The children's groups tailor their message for the X-box generation of kids. The small group is kept exciting and relevant, and creates in the children a desire to know God.

Youth Small Groups

Youth small groups have been tremendous![1] Young people who get involved in small-group leadership grow spiritually themselves as they reach out to others. When our daughter Katrina was 15 years old, she began to serve as an assistant leader in a youth small group that met in our home. It gave her the opportunity to grow in the Lord and develop leadership skills that will be with her for her entire life.

Other Homogeneous Groups

Some small groups may relate to only businessmen. Their focus is to reach out to other businessmen who need to know Christ. Other groups may have only women, or only men or only singles.

One small group at our church was formed by single women who had a burden for unwed mothers. At each meeting, the women would bring small, practical gifts for a baby and deposit them in the box. After a few weeks of praying, the Lord led an unwed mother to their group and they spent prime prayer time interceding for her and her unborn child. When the child was born, they had a lot of items to give along with their prayers and encouragement. This small group disbanded soon afterward, but those participating knew they had been called by God for this very special time of helping this young woman.

How Many People Should Be in Your Small Group?

New groups only need a few people to start. If two or three gather in His name, He is in their midst! Jesus' small group consisted of 12 disciples. Moses encouraged small groups of 10. An ideal number of adults in a group that meets together consistently seems to be from 10 to 15, especially if they have children in addition to the 10 to 15 adults. Often groups without children can grow a bit larger—maybe 15 to 20 adults. When a group grows to more than 20, the group may reach a saturation level where it becomes too large to be effective.

One of our small groups a few years back grew to more than 80 people in it. That group was larger than the average church in America! But we had to wait until leadership was released for the group to multiply. Eventually it did multiple and reduce in number. The key to starting new groups is leadership. If leadership is not adequately prepared to start a new small group, wait until leaders are properly equipped. People who are involved in small groups without clear leadership often become disillusioned.

When a group becomes large, there's another unforeseen problem. Where do you park all the cars when you meet together? Often the overflow spills onto the side of the street or road and can be a potential problem for neighbors. In this case, we suggest that members carpool whenever possible. Respect for the community must always be observed. Cars should never be parked where they interfere with traffic flow or neighbors' properties.

How Do You Dissolve a Group?

To maintain healthy small groups, the group will eventually need to multiply. Even so, there have been times when a group has been together for quite some time without multiplying and finds it hard to keep an outward focus. They are satisfied with their experiences of mutual support and forget their mission to reach out beyond themselves. The closer I look at my face in the mirror each morning, the more imperfections I see. The same principle applies to the church. If we just sit around and look at each other and forget our mission to reach those who do not yet know Jesus, we can quickly begin to dwell on the imperfections we see in one another. This will inevitably lead us down a road of disillusionment in a small-group setting.

When a leader, and others in the group, senses they have become spiritually stagnant, with no one desiring to multiply another group from the parent one, they often realize they must dissolve or discontinue altogether. It is important to have the pastor involved in the process of a group that dissolves. He has the grace and experience to help the members to quickly find their place in another small group before the enemy can sow seeds of discouragement and confusion into their lives.

When a group dissolves, it takes a period of time for believers to get involved in another group. The local pastor may start a "transition group" that he leads temporarily to support God's people and help them discern their future small-group involvement.

Sometimes a lethargic small group just needs a jump-start. Small-group leaders Brendan and Wanda were thinking about dissolving their group. The six others in the group were scattering, and the couple realized they needed new vision, and new people! "God, do You want us to start in another area, or dissolve the small group?" they asked. God seemed to be telling them to simply keep their home open to others. Before long, the group exploded with five new families visiting, plus children, more than filling their home. The group decided they didn't want to just be another small group. They wanted to "get deep, to be there for each other and to pray and watch God meet our needs." They soon enjoyed watching God work in up-close and personal relationships in their group. When we see the changes and beauty God is bringing about in each individual's life, it gives a sense of excitement and reality to each person's Christianity.

Commissioning

Whenever someone in the small group is going out on a mission trip or into a ministry, or moving to another area, the entire group should have a part in commissioning them out. This commissioning should not take place on the spur of the moment. It should be announced well in advance so that no one is taken by surprise. During the time of commissioning, have the members lay their hands on the person or persons, and as many as are led by the Lord should pray. At this time, prophecy and words of wisdom and knowledge may also be given.

Commissioning is also encouraged when multiplying a new group or when confirming new leaders or assistant leaders from within the group. It's important to communicate with the person coaching the small-group leader and with the local pastor prior to this. If the pastor or spiritual overseer can be involved in the commissioning, it gives the Lord's people a sense of being linked to a movement of God, not just to a small group of people.

Be Sensitive to the Holy Spirit

Small groups need to be in a constant state of growth and change or they can quickly become stagnant. A vision constantly put before the members should be one of reaching out and mentoring others so they can multiply and grow and remain healthy and alive. Above all, as a leader, encourage everyone in the group to be sensitive to hearing what the Holy Spirit is saying for a particular time and situation.

A small group in Canada, sensitive to the burden they were feeling for unsaved relatives and friends, began to pray for these loved ones. Upon returning home after a small-group meeting, one woman found her husband in deep repentance. He told her he was sitting at the kitchen table and found himself under such deep conviction that he fell off his chair, onto the floor, repenting for his backslidden condition. The small group had followed what the Father was doing among them and reaped the fruit of their obedience.

At another small-group meeting, some people were feeling sick, so the leader wisely discerned what the Father wanted to do—to move as a healer. Hands were laid on those who were sick and prayers of faith were verbal-ized (see Jas. 5:16). What happened? The Lord stretched out His hand to heal. After all, this is what the Father wanted to do. They simply gave Him the opportunity.

Questions for Discussion

1. When a specific need of a small-group member is communicated to the leader, what steps can be taken to help meet the need?

2. Why is hospitality so important in small groups?

3. What goals have you established for your small group?

Note
1. For more about youth-oriented small groups, read Brian Sauder and Sarah Mohler, *Youth Cells and Youth Ministry* (Lititz, PA: House to House Publications, 2000).

CHAPTER 11

MISTAKES TO AVOID AS A SMALL-GROUP LEADER

Twenty Major Mistakes We Have Made in Small-Group Ministry Leadership

I'm grateful that we are constantly learning; God keeps teaching us how He can build His kingdom through us if we will listen. He is a creative God and continually gives new insights to His people. As I mentioned at the beginning of this book, we have learned a lot from our mistakes over the years, and we want to share with you what doesn't work in small-group ministry. Among the literally hundreds of learning-curve experiences I could share with you, I have chosen to talk about what I feel are the most important lessons.

1. A Lack of Prayer and Desperation for God

It may seem obvious, but it is critical to acknowledge Jesus in the midst of your small-group meetings. Healthy groups focus on prayer! When there is a fervency in prayer—individually, as a group or as a church—God will cover many of our mistakes. Small groups are prayer centers! They provide a natural prayer chain for the local church. We've found that whenever we have become lax in prayer, small problems have quickly become mountains.

Some years back, I was asked to train small-group leaders at the Vienna Christian Center in Vienna, Austria. Though only a few years old, it became the largest Protestant Church in the nation since the Reformation. It was a small-group church, with small groups scattered throughout the city. After I gave a training seminar, I gave the opportunity for prayer for these new leaders to receive more of the Lord's presence in their lives. One of the men, a diplomat, ran to the front of the room for prayer, desperate and hungry for more of God, and many more with the same desire followed suit. There was a genuine hunger for God among them. They rightly believed that if God doesn't show up, it is all over. We must experience more of the life and presence of Jesus in our lives today than we did last week.

Unfortunately, we often trust structures rather than God. The Lord honors people who are desperate for more of Him in their lives. We cannot continue living on past experiences! We must be desperate for a daily fresh touch from the Lord. We must expect the Lord to fill us with His presence when we come together in His name in our meetings.

Daniel and Rebecca Mbiti, from Machakos, Kenya, started a new church based on small groups several years ago. Daniel worked for a bank during the day and served as a pastor evenings and weekends. Rebecca gave up her job to have more time to minister to the needs of those they served. They went into the villages and homes to pray for the sick, and the Lord healed them. Through these miracles, people give their lives to Christ and willingly open their homes for new small groups. It all started with prayer.

Jesus has called us to meet with Him and worship Him each day. The Lord tells us in John 17:3 that eternal life is to know Him. Our number-one priority must be to know Him personally through time spent with Him each day, or small-group ministry will become just another church program.

Dr. Yonggi Cho has spoken about small groups to thousands of pastors and church leaders in America during the past years. I have heard him say that American pastors are attentive when he speaks on small-group principles, but when he begins to teach on prayer and communion with the Holy Spirit, the pastors put their pencils down and stop taking notes. They lose interest.

Jesus says in Matthew 4:4, "Man shall not live by bread alone, but by every word that proceeds from the mouth of God" (*NKJV*). If we are living on last week's manna, we will begin to get weak and even sick spiritually. Only healthy Christians will have something to give to others. I need a fresh word from the Lord every day. And there is no substitute. We must cultivate our relationship with our Lord Jesus every day.

2. Not Understanding God's Purpose for Your Small Group

Just as there are many different types of cells in our body, there are many different types of cells (small groups) in the Body of Christ. Every small group should ask the question: What is the Father doing among us? Some small groups are called by the Lord to focus on youth, others on women, others on families, still others on businesspersons, while others are called to focus on reaching university students. You need to know who the Lord has called you to.

Additionally, you must remember the Lord's priorities for your small group, which include, in a nutshell: prayer, discipleship and evangelism relationships.

Prayer is your relationship with God.

Discipleship is your relationship with other believers.

Evangelism is your relationship with those who do not yet know Jesus.

3. Forgetting that the Main Purpose of the Small Group Is Outreach

It's a major mistake to allow small groups to lose vision for outreach and evangelism and only concentrate on their own needs! Remember, the church is not a hospital but an army. Armies have medical units for people to get healed, but they are then sent back out to battle. We are called to be fishers of men (see Mark 1:17). In the book of Acts, each day those being saved were added to the church (see Acts 2:47). We are to be witnesses (see Acts 1:8), not partakers of complacent, comfortable, "bless me" meetings.

Don and Jeanni served with a small group in Harrisburg, Pennsylvania. They believed the Lord birthed their group to reach those who did not yet know Jesus. They hosted a Japanese student, Yosiko, enrolled in a local university. Week after week they showed her God's love and prayed for her. A few days before Christmas, Yosiko, who grew up in a Buddhist family, declared to Don and Jeanni, "I have just received a Christmas gift. I have asked Jesus Christ to come into my life." The small group rejoiced with her, baptized her and discipled her. When the time came, they empowered her to go back to Japan. The entire group was changed when they focused outward.

Americans tend to forget why they are involved in small-group community life. The primary purpose for the group is not merely for fellowship but to reach pre-Christians. A small group must focus on reaching people in and beyond their communities, or it becomes ingrown and stagnant.

Constant exhortation, encouragement and training from church leaders to follow through with our commission to reach those who do not know Jesus are vital. Without these things, the law of entropy occurs. When groups are content to stay the same, they subconsciously build walls around themselves, causing others to feel unwelcome. The tendency of all new wineskins is to get old, but bringing new people into the group and multiplying keeps us fresh and alive.

The Bible says, "For this purpose the Son of God was manifested, that He might destroy the works of the devil" (1 John 3:8, *NKJV*). The works of the devil are everywhere. Our communities are filled with broken lives characterized by fear, abuse, broken relationships, perversion, the murdering of unborn children, materialism and lust. Jesus came for the purpose of destroying these works!

We must understand that our heart motivation for being involved in small-group ministry must be the same as that of our Lord Jesus—to destroy the works of the devil. Jesus is the answer to every problem. He is the great Redeemer. He came to restore completely every man, woman and child who will open up their hearts and lives to Him. In Romans 10:14, Paul tells us, "How then shall they call on Him in whom they have not believed?" (*NKJV*). We are commissioned by our Lord Jesus Christ to reach the lost of our generation. Small-group ministry is one of the spiritual tools to assist us in fulfilling this mandate from the Lord.

Jesus told His disciples in Matthew 28 to "go," knowing that all authority had been given to Him in heaven and on earth. He promised to be with them always, just as He will always be with us.

4. A Lack of Flexibility

Flexibility, spontaneity and creativity are vital in the small group. Romans 8:14 says that those who are led by the Spirit are the sons of God. Beware of having a cookie-cutter mentality in small-group ministry. Your task as a small-group leader is to teach, guide, set an example and encourage others so that there is freedom, flexibility and growth in the group. Most people don't like to be told what to do. They want choices.

When we first started small-group ministry, we had only family small groups. Later, we saw the need for homogeneous groups that formed around specific interests, like small groups for youth, businesspersons, families with young children, singles, divorced individuals, and so on. The goal is to transform an interest group into a spiritual community through relationships.

As a leader, you should work to help each member blossom in his or her relationship with the Lord. When each member is fulfilling his or her role, the group will grow in size, strength, love and unity.

5. Building by Geography Rather than by Relationship

At one point, we strongly suggested that people in our church attend a small group in their neighborhood, mostly because it made practical sense to attend the group closest to their home. We soon discovered that people want to attend a small group where they have relationships, and this will not always be the group in closest proximity to their house. The kingdom of God is not built by geography but by relationship! Small groups are built by relationship.

One family felt misplaced in their small group and came to me for assistance. I told them they needed to stay in the group. As a result, they left our church. I finally recognized my mistake and asked for their forgiveness.

Not allowing small-group members to change groups if they don't fit in is unhealthy. We used to take the stance that if people had relationship problems within a small group they had to work it out within the group. But this creates a lot of unnecessary problems. We learned that it is best to allow members to go to a small group where they feel called to attend. People are like pieces to a puzzle. They need to find where they fit. Small-group leaders, too, must have a sense of faith that the pieces of the puzzle fit.

6. Unhealthy Control

For a while, we told our small-group members they should share their needs with their small-group leader first before sharing with a pastor or other person. This was a mistake! Sometimes people are uncomfortable sharing deep problems with their small-group leaders, especially those people who are new to the group. It takes time to build trust. People should share with leaders because they want to, not because they have to. If small-group members do not confide in you as their leader, remain secure, knowing that the members will come around when they have established a relationship of trust with you.

Another way that unhealthy control can raise its ugly head is when small-group leaders do not encourage leaders from within their group to step out and start another small group. Remember, our God is a God of multiplication!

7. Too Much Emphasis on the Meeting and Not Enough on the Relationships

In Acts 2:42-47, the New Testament church was filled with life and fellowship, not just meetings. The key is not so much what happens in small-group meetings but what happens after the meeting and during the week.

Leaders who say, "People don't come to our meetings," usually are not building relationships with the people outside the group meetings. After or between meetings, people often share intimately and pray for each other informally as they relate one to one.

As well, keep the meetings from getting too rigid. If you always pray at a certain time, worship at a certain time, have a teaching and share at a certain time and then have a snack, you lose spontaneity. Your small group becomes a mini version of Sunday morning church. This is not the purpose of the small group. In the small group, everyone's gift can be used, not just the gifts of a few paid church staff.

8. Expecting Every Assistant Leader to Be a Future Leader

The text of 1 Corinthians 12:11 indicates that God distributes gifts as He wills. It is important to have as many assistant leaders as possible so you can train them to be future leaders. Assistant leaders receive from God a healthy stewardship for the small group; however, not every assistant leader will become a leader. Some assistant leaders have a supportive gift. Encourage them in the gift the Lord has given to them.

9. Lack of Training for New Believers on the Basics of Christianity

New believers need a systematic biblical foundation in their lives, like a first-grade through twelfth-grade education. Attending a small group and a Sunday church meeting alone will not give new believers proper training. They need to systematically study the Bible. We recommend using a biblical foundation course like my 12-book *Biblical Foundation* series or my 2-book series entitled *Discovering the Basic Truths of Christianity* and *Building Your Life on the Basic Truths of Christianity*. These books cover the major biblical tenets including faith, baptism, knowing Jesus as Savior, forgiveness, repentance from sin, the resurrection, and many other biblical doctrines.[1]

10. Lack of Preparation for Meetings (a Lack of Structure)

Romans 12:11 tells us to not be lagging in diligence. Without preparation, the small group becomes a social club. We honor people by preparing and then being open to change as the Holy Spirit leads. A complete lack of structure will eventually frustrate people! Sometimes we say we are obeying the Holy Spirit, but in reality, it is laziness.

11. Not Expecting the Small Group to Multiply

When we stop believing our small group will eventually multiply, our group begins to stagnate. As a small-group leader, speak about multiplication in your meetings. Pray about multiplication. Expect it to happen! All members must realize they can multiply their life through passing on their faith to others.

A key to small-group multiplication is to serve the group as a facilitator. As a leader, you are a facilitator. Jesus and the early apostles constantly facilitated the delegation of responsibility to others. Others learn by doing. In 1 Corinthians 1:14, Paul delegated baptism to others. A wise leader will work himself out of a job. We need to be careful to delegate but not abdicate (we still have the responsibility). Planning outreaches, picnics, meals for shut-ins and many other small-group responsibilities can often be delegated to others. And they learn by doing.

12. Lack of Clear Leadership

Judges 5:2 tells us that when leaders lead, the people freely volunteer. If God's appointed leaders do not blow a clear trumpet sound, someone else will! In our experience, whenever we did not stress the need for God-given leadership in small groups, we stopped reaching the unsaved and the group eventually stagnated.

Harold Eberle, in his book *The Complete Wineskin*, explains it like this:

> After observing many, many churches, I can personally tell you that no matter what form of government a church claims to have, there is always one person who openly or quietly holds the greatest influence over the church. Setting up the proper government is never a matter of keeping it out of the hands of one person, but putting it into the hands of God's person.[2]

We have found this same principle applies to small-group leadership. Every small group needs a leader called by God, an assistant leader (or assistant leaders), and a core leadership team to serve with him. Obviously this may take time to build, but this is the goal. Wise leaders also will have a heart that is open to listen to what God is saying through His people. But families, both natural and spiritual, need parents—leaders to lead them.

13. Compromising the God-given Vision

Galatians 1:10 tells us that if we are a slave to men (seeking to please others), we cannot be a servant of Christ. Beware of the migratory flock that migrates from church to church, and from small group to small group. Sometimes these persons will pressure you to return to old ways of doing things. It is easy to go back to a "meeting mentality" or a "Bible study mentality" rather than a "spiritual family mentality." Paul the apostle, in Acts 26:19, told King Agrippa, "I was not disobedient to the vision from heaven" (*NIV*). We must be obedient to the vision the Lord has given to us for our small group, and not become sidetracked by the many opinions around us. Every time I swayed from what I knew the Lord had called me to do, eventually our group began to stagnate. I needed to repent and go back to the vision that I knew the Lord had given to our leadership team. Small-group ministry can take a lot of hard work to stay on course, but it is so rewarding!

14. Emphasis on Teaching Methods Rather than on the Word of God

If we only teach our own ideas or new methods in our small groups, believers will trust in the wisdom of man rather than in the Word of God (see 2 Tim. 3:16-17). For example, if we teach small-group multiplication from our vision rather than from the Word, it becomes a program with no life.

Make it clear that the small group is a spiritual family whose desire is to release its children to start their own families (see 1 John 2:12-14); otherwise, small-group ministry becomes a fad or the latest church program.

At different times, we have picked up methods from others without understanding the values behind the methods. Each time this has caused a problem. If we understand the values being taught, the methods will follow. Are we doing what Jesus has really called us to do? Or are we copying a good idea from others?

The first time we went to visit the world's largest church in Korea, we learned that the Korean believers were multiplying their small groups every six months. As the senior pastor, I came back to America and asked our small-group leaders to do the same, and we burned out the small-group leaders. I had to repent to them for this mistake. Glean ideas from others, then lay it all before the Lord and ask Him what to do. Every culture is different! Understand why they do what they do! The same principles and values apply everywhere but are worked out differently in each culture.

15. A Lack of Discipleship

Unless we have a clear understanding that making disciples is near the top of God's priority list, small-group ministry will be just another religious program.

Jesus had a vision to revolutionize the world—person to person, house to house. Out of the multitudes of His followers, He appointed only 12 to be His disciples. By living closely with them, day in and day out, He gave them intense training, demonstrated His miraculous power, explained His parables and answered their questions.

The Bible gives many examples of discipleship. Paul, the apostle, took young Timothy with him as a disciple (see Acts 16). Later, Timothy was sent out to do the same: take the truths that he had learned from Paul and impart them to others (see 2 Tim. 2:2). Moses had Joshua as his disciple for 40 years, preparing Joshua for leadership. Elijah found Elisha and became his mentor. The list goes on and on. The Lord is restoring the truth of loving discipleship to His church today. He has called us to make disciples.

Having a small-group meeting every week will not automatically make disciples according to the pattern of Jesus. We learned this the hard way. Discipleship is often one on one or one on two at Starbucks, talking out real-life issues and how Jesus changes us daily as we trust His Word and do not lean on our own emotions and thinking. The small group is the place where we can initially find these relationships, but the actual discipleship often happens mostly outside of the small-group meeting.

16. A Lack of God-given Goals

Goals are important! The Bible tells us, "I press on toward the goal to win the prize for which God has called me heavenward in Christ Jesus" (Phil. 3:14, *NIV*) and "Therefore I do not run like a man running aimlessly; I do not fight like a man beating the air" (1 Cor. 9:26, *NIV*).

A goal is a statement of faith, a course of action. Jesus is returning to this earth. It is a goal that He has fixed. God has goals for His body (the church) and for each of us individually. We, like the apostle Paul, must run toward those goals that God has set before us.

Every small group and every small-group leader needs clear, attainable goals. Ask the Lord what goals He wants you to set for yourself as a small-group leader. God's plan is to use each of us to set goals under the Holy Spirit's direction to change the world in which we live.

If you have a goal to pray for each member of your small group, don't just say you will pray. Set a specific goal that is clear, measurable and attainable. For example, decide to pray one minute a day for each person and progress from there.

As you set goals as a small group, try to involve as many persons in the group as possible in the process. This way the whole small group will feel a sense of responsibility for these goals to be reached. If you implement new goals and ideas too fast, the group may feel lost.

I grew up as a farm boy. During the fall of every year we dug our sweet potatoes for the winter. We placed these sweet potatoes in baskets and put them on a truck. Then came the excitement of driving the farm truck filled with sweet potatoes from the field to the house. Driving that old pickup truck was a real art. We had to round the corners very slowly or we would upset the whole load of sweet potatoes. In the same way, when we make spiritual decisions that will affect others, we need to give them enough time to know that they are a part of the decision-making process so that they don't "fall off the truck." Discuss new ideas with those in your small group before making final decisions. You are called as a team to see the kingdom of God built together.

Get away to pray so that the goals you set are not natural goals, but goals that are birthed by the Holy Spirit. Perhaps the Lord will make it clear to you that you should believe Him to see a family saved within the next two months. Or perhaps you will have as a goal to spend a certain amount of time together in prayer each week. Ask the Lord for a practical goal regarding small-group multiplication. The old saying is true: If you fail to plan, you plan to fail!

One word of caution concerning goals: To not reach your goal may not necessarily be failure. On the other hand, to reach your goal may not be success. Ministry to the Lord and to people must be the ultimate goal!

In the early days of our church we set multiplication goals for small groups based more on mathematical calculations rather than on Holy Spirit-led guidance. This was a big mistake.

God is concerned about our motivations. We must build only by the Holy Spirit's direction. Because we believe goals are important, we encourage a healthy small group to have a goal to multiply approximately once each year. This goal is not bondage, but freedom. If we aim at nothing, we hit nothing; goals must be birthed in prayer and set by the Holy Spirit's direction.

17. A Lack of Accountable Connection to the Body of Christ

In the early days of our church, a team of church leaders from a local denomination gave us oversight. Later on, as we experienced success because our small groups were multiplying and our church was rapidly growing, we didn't feel we needed to have people outside of ourselves to help us. We felt we could handle things ourselves. Pride had crept in. We had no outside court of appeal. This was a major mistake. When we had leadership problems and conflicting personalities and differences of vision, we had nowhere to turn. We learned the hard way, and God humbled us and placed spiritual fathers in our lives.

Connect with others you trust—those who will encourage the vision the Lord has given to you and who will speak the truth in love to you. In the Old Testament there were 12 tribes, and yet they were all the children of Israel. God has raised up many families of churches (tribes) today. I am convinced that it is best for small groups to be connected to other small groups and for them to be linked to spiritual leaders in a local church. I also believe that churches find spiritual protection when they are connected to other churches and spiritual leadership for accountability. The early churches in the New Testament looked to the early apostles for guidance and spiritual protection.

18. A Lack of God-given Vision

The Bible tells us clearly that without a vision the people will perish (see Prov. 29:18). However, although a clearly written and articulated vision is very important and advantageous, remember that those in our small groups need to be honored as people.

Jesus had a personal vision. Therefore, He endured the cross (see Heb. 12:2). Every business, every family, every person, every church should have a vision. Just as those who are married verbalize their commitment to their spouse by saying, "I love you," we need to verbalize our commitment to support the vision that the Lord has given to us as a local church.

A friend who is a church consultant told me that vision must be spoken and communicated publicly at least 20 times per year. Habakkuk 2:2 tells us to write the vision down so others can run with us. Take care, however, that you do not exalt the small group's vision or church's vision above Jesus. God is the ultimate visionary, and we are created in His image. We are given the potential to dream and have visions. But if we shift our primary focus from Jesus to our vision, we'll become ensnared.

Many times during the past years I have had to refocus my vision and energies on my relationship with Jesus and then to the vision that the Lord has given to us as a church. When we begin to emphasize the vision that the Lord has given us more than we emphasize our relationship with Jesus, we create an idol in our hearts (see 1 John

5:21). Even a God-inspired vision, when given preeminence above the Lord Himself, will cause us to stumble.

It is important for the small-group leader to both understand and articulate the vision of the local church and then share it with the small group regularly. It has been said that every church must have a compelling vision (who you really are), a defined mission (what your purpose is), and a well-laid-out plan (how you are going to do it).

19. Emphasizing House to House and Excluding "the Temple"

Both celebration (temple ministry) and small group (house-to-house ministry) are important! There may be times to place more emphasis on house-to-house ministry, and other times to place more emphasis on temple ministry. At times we get off balance, but that is okay. Every time you take a step, you are off balance. But if you never take a step, you never go anywhere. Each local church needs to find a balance of how often they meet in small groups and how often they meet in "temple ministry." The small groups then meet in accordance with the vision of the local church or ministry they are a part of.

20. Pride

A common pitfall and trap to avoid in small groups and house churches is pride.[3] Small groups are not the panacea for today's ailing church. If those of us who are called to small groups take a superior attitude, the Bible tells us we will fall. We need to be very careful not to develop an independent and isolationist spirit. Small groups and house churches may also fall into the pitfall of heresy if they are prideful and exclusive and unwilling to work with others.

These are only 20 of the hundreds of mistakes we have made in small-group ministry over a period of many years. We share them with you so that you are not destined to do the same. May God give you grace to not make these mistakes. But if you do, stop and acknowledge the mistake, repent, receive forgiveness and move on. Don't waste your mistakes; learn from them.

In the final chapter, we'll take a step of faith together.

Questions for Discussion

1. Someone once said that a mistake isn't a mistake unless you don't learn from it. Which of these mistakes have you personally made in small-group ministry, and what have you learned?

2. Why is it important to build small groups by relationship instead of focusing too much on the meetings?

3. Why should small groups have an accountable connection with the local Body of Christ?

Notes
  1. Larry Kreider, 12-book series: *Biblical Foundations* (Lititz, PA: House to House Publications); Larry Kreider, 2-book series: *Discovering the Basic Truths of Christianity* and *Building Your Life on the Basic Truths of Christianity* (Shippensburg, PA: Destiny Image Publishers, 2009).

2. Harold Eberle, *The Complete Wineskin* (Enumclaw, WA: Winepress Publishing, 1989), pp. 144-145.
3. For more about house churches, read *Starting a House Church* by Larry Kreider and Floyd McClung (Ventura, CA: Regal Books, 2007).

CHAPTER 12

STEP OUT IN FAITH

Trust God for His Help, Refuse to Quit and Prepare for the Future

During the week after September 11, 2001, I got on five different planes traveling to five cities in the United States. Airports were deserted, and passengers were scared. As I boarded a flight from Denver, Colorado, to Washington, DC, I could feel a cloud of fear settle on my fellow passengers.

Within moments, however, something changed. Before the plane pushed away from the ramp, the pilot greeted us: "Let's talk about what happened last week," he said with confidence in his voice. "The Constitution of the United States says, 'We the people.' We are in this together. If someone on this plane claims to have a weapon or a bomb and tries something stupid, there are 100 of us on this plane and 1 of him. If you have a computer on your lap, throw it at him! Use your pillow or blanket to protect yourself, and jump on top of anyone who claims to have a weapon. Push him to the floor of the airplane, and we will bring him to justice."

He paused for a few seconds, allowing our minds to take it all in. "Now, shake your neighbor's hand, ask him if he is married, ask him how many children he has, ask where he works, and get to know him." Within moments, the entire atmosphere on the plane changed. I believe it changed from fear to faith. The pilot was encouraging us to build relationships. Relationships, in turn, encourage trust, which builds faith. That pilot was on to something.

Of course, it is something that you probably know already if you are involved in small groups! Small groups are greenhouses where relationships flourish and faith is built. Building relationships one at a time and mentoring others in their faith builds strong Christians.

John Wesley and George Whitefield were famous preachers who lived during the eighteenth century. Both of them belonged to the same "Holy Club" at Oxford University. Most believe that Whitefield was a better preacher than Wesley. Benjamin Franklin once calculated that Whitefield could easily preach to a crowd of 30,000 people—without a microphone.

Whitefield probably recorded more decisions for Christ than Wesley because of the huge crowds he attracted. Yet, there were some major differences between the two. At the end of his life, George Whitefield said this: "My brother Wesley acted wisely—the souls that were awakened under his ministry he joined in classes, and thus preserved the fruits of his labor. This I neglected and my people are a rope of sand." Wesley took the time to disciple his converts in small groups or "classes." Whitefield simply preached to crowds, and many fell away because they didn't get the one-on-one encouragement they needed to grow in their spiritual lives.

Understanding "Spiritual Mathematics" in Small-Group Ministry

By now you know that only God can grow a healthy small group. You totally rely on and trust Him for the increase. In the same way that pupils in school learn to add, subtract, multiply and divide, as a leader of a small group, you need to understand spiritual mathematics. Let's look at these four areas and the test that comes with each area.

Addition

Expect people to be added to your small group! Talk about it and pray about it as a group. Without faith it is impossible to please the Lord (see Heb. 11:6). Jesus calls us to be fishers of men (see Mark 1:17), but we must properly prepare to go fishing. God's will is for your group to grow.

Who does God want to add to your group? He wants to add from at least five groups of people:

1. New converts—God desires all to be saved and to come to the knowledge of the truth (see 1 Tim. 2:1-4)
2. New people moving to your area
3. Christians who have no church home
4. Babies born into families within the small group
5. Misplaced believers in the Body of Christ—some believers are in the wrong small group, and others are in the wrong congregation

Can we believe for our group to grow? *The test of addition is a test of faith.*

Subtraction

According to 2 Timothy 4:10-12, there were those who left Paul's "small group" for various reasons. When people leave, as much as possible, commission them out. This destroys speculation. Here are some of the reasons why people leave:

- Those who are "sent out" to missions or college. They can still be a part of the group as you pray for them and encourage them, but for a season they are no longer physically with you.

- Those who are sent out to another church or another small group. Don't take it personally. Allow the Lord to place people in His Body (see 1 Cor. 12:18).

- Those who just leave or disappear. Jesus left the 99 to search for the 1. Pursue them to find out what is happening in their lives.

- Those who backslide (see Jas. 5:19-20). Again, don't assume you know why they left. Talk to them to find out and communicate clearly with the rest of the group.

- Those who experience church discipline due to unrepentant sin. Church elders should help process this scripturally (see Gal. 5:19-21, Matt. 18:15-17 and 1 Cor. 5).

Are we threatened when someone leaves our small group, or is our security in Christ? *The test of subtraction is a test of security.*

Multiplication
Believe God for your small group to grow and multiply as new people come to Christ, even though you do not

see progress today. Yet, never forget the Lord's most focused goal for your life: to make you more like Jesus.

The character of Christ is developed in us through the process of the trials and disappointments of life. We must trust Him and His Word rather than our present circumstances. Anyone can be excited when things go well. What about when our expectations are not met? What happens to you when your group goes for a season without anyone coming to Christ, or doesn't multiply as often as you had projected, or people seem to leave your group for the wrong reasons? Continue to pray and to believe, but be sure to not miss the Lord's higher way and higher thoughts for your life.

When crops do not receive the blessing of rain for a season, the drought forces their roots to go deep for moisture. A season of spiritual drought just might be the proper environment for our spiritual roots to go down deeper into Him. The Lord is calling us to complete dependency on Him as we persevere during the process of life. One of the most effective means of spiritual warfare is simply to not quit!

In Mark 4:20, Jesus speaks of seed reproducing 30-, 60- and 100-fold. We need to expect multiplication to happen in our small group. Acts 9:31 says the early disciples walked in the fear of the Lord, the comfort of the Holy Spirit, and were multiplied. Let's not hold on to those the Lord has placed in our small groups, but instead, train them to give away.

The farmer sows his seeds in faith. See your group through eyes of faith. Prepare the field/soil for future multiplication. See future leaders through the eyes of faith. Samuel saw David through eyes of faith. Barnabas saw Saul through eyes of faith. Jesus saw His disciples through eyes of faith. Pour your time into faithful people (see 2 Tim. 2:2). Encourage future leaders. Let them know they can do it (see Heb. 3:13). We all need encouragement.

Give future leaders responsibility (one step at a time). Break responsibility down into simple tasks so people understand it. It is always best to put this in writing. And remember, the two most important responsibilities of a small-group leader are (1) to pray, and (2) to train future leaders.

Beware of tunnel vision. See your group through the eyes of faith.

- Believers multiply by leading others to Christ.
- Small groups multiply by starting new groups.
- Churches multiply by starting new churches.

The test of multiplication is a test of releasing others.

Division

Division is the enemy's most powerful strategy. Nearly every family, society, nation and church that has been destroyed was destroyed from within. Even David had division with his son Absalom. Pray against a divisive spirit and for unity and wisdom in your small group (see Jas. 1:5).

Be careful to not receive an accusation unless there are two or three witnesses (see 1 Tim. 5:19-20). Titus 3:10 says that we should "reject a divisive man after the first and second admonition" (*NKJV*).

What if you are facing division in your small group? Words of division sow seeds of doubt about the group and the leader. As a leader, face your fears and confront the divisive individual in love. Be sure to bathe the process in prayer and speak with compassion. Maintaining a godly attitude is extremely important (see Gal. 6:1-2). Follow the steps of reconciliation that Jesus gave us in Matthew 18:15-19. Division must be confronted. It will not just go away. Get help from your pastor if you are dealing with gossip and division in your small group. The Lord has given them the grace to handle it in a godly manner.

Remember, unity does not mean total agreement. Unity comes from knowing we are called to serve together. Small-group members should appeal to their leader and then back his or her decision. The Moravians taught that "in essentials: unity, in nonessentials: diversity, in all things: charity."[1]

Will we respond in loving boldness to situations that could hinder the group and our church?

The test of division is a test of character.

As a small-group leader you may have to take these four tests various times while serving your small group. But remember, with the Lord we never fail His tests; we just keep taking them over again until we pass!

Back to the Book of Acts

I love to read the book of Acts. It seems like everywhere the apostles went there was either a revival or a riot. Paul and Silas went to Philippi and cast a demon out of a fortune-teller. Her masters were irate and threw Paul and Silas into prison. So they started singing hymns and the Lord sent an earthquake that opened the prison doors. The jailer was so shook up that he was going to take his life, but Paul quickly assured him that the prisoners were all still there in the prison. Let's pick up on the story.

And he brought them out and said, "Sirs, what must I do to be saved?" So they said, "Believe on the Lord Jesus Christ, and you will be saved, you and your *household*." Then they spoke the word of the Lord to him and to all who were in his *house*. And he took them the same hour of the night and washed their stripes. And immediately he and all his family were baptized. Now when he had brought them into his *house*, he set food before them; and he rejoiced, having believed in God with all his *household* (Acts 16:30-34, *NKJV,* emphasis added).

These guys were amazing! Paul and Silas had just experienced imprisonment, a beating and an earthquake. Yet they were prepared to experience a move of God, in the home of the jailer. It all happened "underground," in a home.

I believe the next revival could happen from house to house. Have you experienced a spiritual prison or a spiritual earthquake in your life during the recent past? We should expect a move of God in our homes and in the homes of those the Lord will bring into our lives.

Be Willing to Change

The only thing that is constant on this earth is the Word of God, and *change*! It is a bit unnerving, but true. As we truly follow the leading of the Holy Spirit, we will continue to change. Our small groups will change, and each of us will continue to change as we mature in Christ.

Change is hard for most of us. But if we are going to grow and mature, we must constantly be ready to embrace change. The change that takes place when a small group multiplies is not easy for the majority of us. But as leaders, we must help others get ready for the change. It often helps God's people when they realize that even leaders do not necessarily feel like changing, but they understand that change is simply a part of normal church life.

We are naturally resistant to change. Human nature has always resisted change. Building the church through small groups requires a lot of flexibility and change. But then, that is what life is all about. One of my friends from YWAM once told me, "Either we can keep everything neat and organized, or we can continue to allow the Lord to birth new things among us. Birthing is messy and painful, but there is life!" I vote for life. How about you?

Seeing others come to Jesus and helping people step by step in their Christian walk—that's real life! And it happens so effectively in the small-group setting. The power of God is released as small groups learn to do the work of the kingdom of God and stay open to change.

Preparing for the Future

Now is the time to prepare for the future. The church must be built from house to house! The Lord used the early disciples to focus on ministering from house to house (see Acts 20:20). Two hundred years ago, John Wesley, the founder of the Methodist church, and thousands of small-group leaders changed a whole generation for Christ. Now it's our turn.

California redwood trees are known to be some of the largest trees in the world. The secret of their ability to stand tall is not in their deep root system. The secret is in the fact that the roots of the trees are interconnected with the roots of the trees growing around them. They are interdependent. Each one needs the others. And as small-group leaders from many different churches and denominations, we need each other. Let's continue to learn from one another as God builds His church from house to house.

I hope this book has been a blessing to you. May you experience the Lord's grace and His presence in your life as you obey Him as a small-group leader. Let's live with the expectancy that we will experience the life of the New Testament church found in the book of Acts in our small groups! The best is yet to come!

Questions for Discussion

1. How has spiritual mathematics worked in your small group?

2. Describe a time when change was difficult for your group.

3. How do you encourage flexibility in the small group?

Note
1. J. E. Hutton, *A History of the Moravian Church* (London: Moravian Publication Office, 1909), p. 434.

ALSO BY
LARRY KREIDER

STARTING A HOUSE CHURCH
A New Model for Living Out Your Faith
Larry Kreider & Floyd McClung
ISBN 978.08307.53650
ISBN 08307.43650

AUTHENTIC SPIRITUAL MENTORING
Nurturing Younger Believers Toward
Spiritual Maturity
Larry Kreider
ISBN 978.08307.44138
ISBN 08307.44134

GOD IS ALWAYS SPEAKING, BUT WE'RE NOT ALWAYS LISTENING

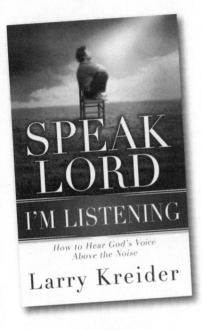

SPEAK LORD, I'M LISTENING
Larry Kreider
ISBN 978.08307.46125
ISBN 08307.46129

A voice from a flaming bush in the desert . . . thunder and lightning trumpeting from a cloud of smoke . . . a donkey addressing her disobedient master . . . a blinding light on the dusty road to Damascus. When you read these famous biblical descriptions of God's voice, you might be tempted to believe that He no longer speaks to His children today. Yet God is speaking to you, every day and in a myriad of ways. *Speak, Lord, I'm Listening* presents more than 50 ways to hear the voice of God and recognize His activity in and through your life. Although He may most often speak through His Word, circumstances, other Christians and commonsense wisdom, don't make the mistake of putting God in a box! His voice is not limited by human rules and preferences, and He promises to make Himself known if you call on Him. Let the principles in *Speak, Lord, I'm Listening* tune your ears to hear God's voice, for there is nothing more important than learning to listen.